WASHINGTON, D.C.

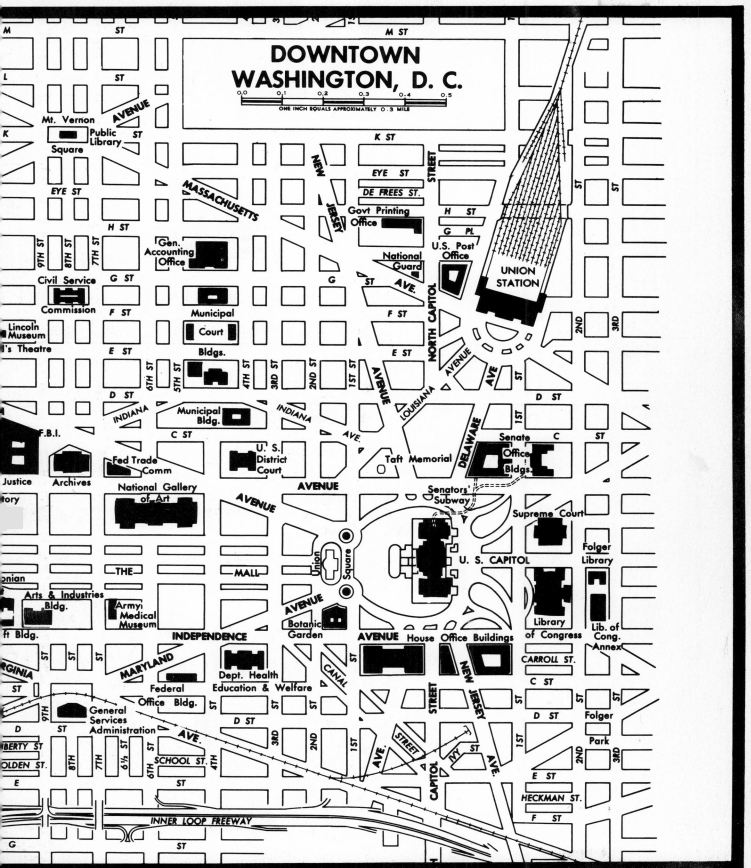

DOWNTOWN
WASHINGTON, D. C.

0.0   0.1   0.2   0.3   0.4   0.5

ONE INCH EQUALS APPROXIMATELY 0.3 MILE

BEAUTIFUL
WASHINGTON, D.C.

BEAUTIFUL WASHINGTON, D.C.

A Picture Story of the Nation's Capital

GENE GURNEY

with special photography by HAROLD WISE

CROWN PUBLISHERS, INC., NEW YORK

ACKNOWLEDGMENTS

IN ADDITION TO PHOTOGRAPHY by Harold Wise, this book contains photographs from other sources. They are listed below and to all of them the author extends his appreciation.

American Airlines
American University
Architect of the Capitol
Arena Stage
Atomic Energy Commission
Catholic University of America
The Corcoran Gallery of Art
Danish Embassy
Department of Agriculture
Department of Defense
Department of Health, Education, and Welfare
Department of Housing and Urban Development
Department of Labor
Department of State
Department of the Army
Department of the Navy
District of Columbia Stadium
Embassy of Finland
Federal Aviation Administration
Federal Bureau of Investigation
Federal Republic of Germany Embassy
The Folger Shakespeare Library
French Embassy
The George Washington University
Georgetown University News Service
Government Printing Office

Howard University
Howard University Art Department
Italian Embassy
Kennedy Center for the Performing Arts
Library of Congress
The Madison Hotel
Masonic Lodge of Alexandria
The Mayflower
Mount Vernon Ladies' Association
National Aeronautics and Space Administration
National Geographic Society
National Historical Wax Museum and Tourist Center
National Park Service
National Society, Daughters of the American Revolution
National Trust for Historic Preservation
Naval Historical Foundation
Norwegian Embassy
The Phillips Collection
Post Office Department
Royal Netherlands Embassy
The Shoreham Hotel and Motor Inn
Smithsonian Institution
Veterans Administration
Washington Convention and Visitors Bureau
The Washington Hilton
The White House

CONTENTS

BEAUTIFUL
WASHINGTON, D.C.

Washington's public buildings stand
out in its otherwise low skyline as befits
a city whose chief business is government. Building height is regulated by
law to keep other structures from over-
shadowing the Capitol.

1

THE FEDERAL CITY

GEORGE WASHINGTON PERSONALLY SELECTED the site of the nation's Capital. He made his choice in January, 1791, some six months after Congress had authorized him to choose a location "not exceeding 10 miles square" somewhere along the Potomac River. In addition to choosing a site, the first President was instructed to acquire the necessary land and to appoint a building commission to oversee the construction of the new Federal city.

Congress had passed the so-called Residence Act after a long and bitter debate that threatened to tear the young Republic apart as northern and southern interests contended for the proposed "Federal town." While meeting in Princeton and Trenton, New Jersey, and in New York City, the Continental Congress struggled with the problem, at one time seriously considering a proposal to build two Federal towns, one on the Potomac and one on the Delaware River. It was not until the Constitution had been ratified that the First Congress of the United States, meeting in New York City, resolved the Federal town problem by agreeing to a compromise arranged by Alexander Hamilton and Thomas Jefferson. In return for the selection of the Potomac region as the location of the coveted Federal town, southern congressmen agreed to vote for a bill authorizing the Federal Government to assume the Revolutionary War debts of the individual states, a measure strongly

favored by many northern congressmen.

In his role as the land agent for Congress, Washington, already familiar with the Potomac region, considered various locations for the Federal city, from Conococheague Creek, about eighty miles above the present Washington, to an area about ten miles farther down the river. He chose a beautiful part of the Potomac Valley where the river becomes wide and tidal and is joined by a smaller stream, the Anacostia River.

As soon as he had selected a site, Washington appointed a three-man building commission and hired Andrew Ellicott to survey the land. He chose Major Pierre Charles L'Enfant to lay out the new town.

L'Enfant, a French engineer who had served with the Continental Army during the Revolutionary War, proposed to create a Federal city "magnificent enough to grace a great nation." In less than a year he was dismissed as a failure, but his ideas for a magnificent city, as expressed in his plan for Washington, have shaped the development of the Capital.

It was L'Enfant who selected imposing Jenkins Hill as the location of the Federal House, as he called the Capitol. He laid out a broad avenue, stipulating that it be 160 feet wide, to connect the Federal House with the President's House a mile away. That thoroughfare became Pennsylvania Avenue. He overlaid other broad avenues on a rectangular street pattern and designated ample sites for public buildings.

L'Enfant's generous allocation of land for streets and public buildings led to his downfall. At Washington's request, the local landowners had agreed to sell land that would be needed for public buildings for about sixty-six dollars an acre, considerably less than they thought it was worth, while land needed for streets was to be given to the government free of charge. When they saw L'Enfant's plan, with its wide streets and large sites for public buildings, they protested loudly. They had not expected to provide the land for streets that were 100 or 110 feet wide, avenues that measured 160 feet across, and one grand 400-foot avenue that was a mile long!

Then L'Enfant tore down a manor house that Daniel Carroll was building, claiming that the house did not fit into his plan for the Federal city, and, furthermore, that it blocked one of his vistas. Unfortunately, Daniel Carroll was not only a wealthy landowner, he was one of the three commissioners who were technically in charge of the Federal city as well. L'Enfant had already angered the commissioners by refusing to let them see his plans. Now they went to George Washington, and the President was forced to dismiss L'Enfant, who angrily refused an offer of $2,500 and a free lot for the work that he had already done.

When L'Enfant died in poverty in 1825, only a small portion of his proposals for the Federal city had been adopted, mainly the location of the President's House, the Capitol, and the city's main streets. But his plan for Washington was preserved and many years later it was revived.

After L'Enfant's dismissal, the planning and building of the Federal city continued, but progress was slow. When the government moved to Washington in 1800, it was still a raw village with unfinished buildings and muddy streets.

During the War of 1812, much of what had been accomplished in the Federal city was destroyed. British soldiers and marines entered the undefended Capital on August 24, 1814, after defeating American troops at Bladensburg, Maryland. Before they left the next day, the British had burned the President's House, the Capitol, and a score of public buildings.

The fire forced the Federal Government into temporary quarters during a period of rebuilding after which the slow growth of the city continued. The Baltimore and Ohio Railway reached Washington in 1835; the first telegraph line in 1844. But in 1846 Congress voted to return to Virginia the part of the ten-square-mile District of Columbia that lay south of the Potomac River. It seemed unlikely that the land would ever be needed for the Capital.

The Civil War changed Washington from a village into a city as soldiers and civilians crowded into the Capital. With Confederate forces coming dangerously close at times, Washington's parks became camping grounds while churches and other buildings were pressed into service as hospitals. The city itself was ringed by a series of forts. At one of them, Fort Stevens, President Lincoln came under enemy fire as he watched Union troops drive back the forces of General Jubal Early. Some of the forts, including Fort Stevens, have been preserved. Others are now small parks.

Post–Civil War Washington continued to grow in a haphazard fashion and during the early 1870's the city embarked on its first big civic improvement program under the leadership of Alexander Shepherd, vice president and executive officer of the board of public works. He paved the city's streets and lighted them, built miles of sewers, improved the water supply and attempted to beautify the Capital by building parks and planting trees. Within a few years the appearance of the city was much improved, but in the process the District debt rose to $22,000,000, $12,000,000 more than the legal limit.

Perhaps for that reason, the next attempt to regenerate Washington did not take place until 1901, when Congress named Senator James McMillan of Michigan to head a commission to study the future growth of the Capital. McMillan, in turn, appointed a committee to work out "plans for the development and improvement of the park system of the District of Columbia." The committee, interpreting its assignment broadly, went back to L'Enfant's original design for Washington and recommended that the future development of the Capital proceed according to a plan that was an enlargement and extension of the one that L'Enfant had prepared a century earlier.

Although the McMillan Commission's report was never officially adopted by Congress, it was instrumental in clearing the area west of the Capitol that L'Enfant had intended to be an open plaza leading to the Washington Monument, thus restoring the Mall to the important place that L'Enfant had envisioned for it and, in general, directing the development of Washington along the lines that he had intended.

Washington is now undergoing another period of rejuvenation. New freeways and expressways are cutting through the city, old buildings of wood and masonry are coming down and new ones of steel and glass are going up. A serious attempt is under way to make the Capital more beautiful, not only in its parks, but everywhere. With these changes, as with all the others that have taken place over the years and those planned for the future, Washington is moving closer to the realization of L'Enfant's hope that it become a city magnificent enough to grace a great nation.

Trees line Washington's streets, even the main thoroughfares. This is Fourteenth Street, with the Potomac River in the background.

THE CITY of WASHINGTON in 1800.

Published Nov. 19 1804, by Richard Phillips 71 St Pauls Church Yd.

An engraving made in 1800, the year that the government moved to Washington, shows only a few buildings in the new Federal city. One unhappy government official wrote: "There are few houses in any one place, and most of them small, miserable huts, which present an awful contrast to the public buildings."

Flames engulf the President's House (*left*), and British officers direct the burning of other public buildings in this engraving entitled "Capture of the City of Washington." While little private property was destroyed, a combined Post Office and Patent Office was the only government building to escape the flames on August 24 and 25, 1814.

RAPIN'S HISTORY OF ENGLAND.

L'Enfant's plan
for the city of Washington.

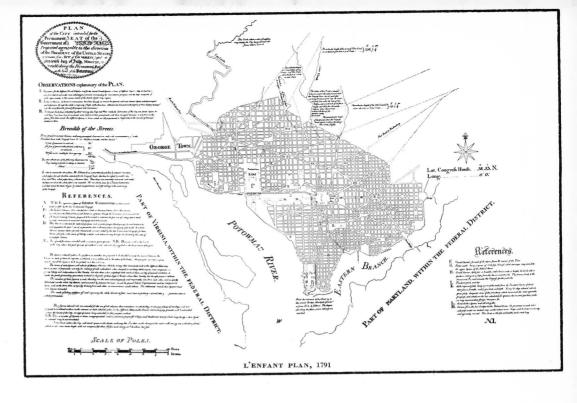

L'ENFANT PLAN, 1791

City of Washington
beyond the Navy Yard.
Aquatint by W. J. Bennett,
1834, after G. Cooke.

VIEW OF WASHINGTON.

Published and sold by E. Sachse & Co. Baltimore Md.

Funeral of Col. Vosburg

Washington became a military headquarters during the Civil War. Here, a military funeral procession passes the unfinished Capitol en route to one of the railroad stations, then located at the edge of the Mall.

Opposite top
Although most of Washington's earliest inns and hotels were located on Pennsylvania Avenue between the Capitol and Seventh Street, this 1839 engraving of the avenue at Seventh Street shows an almost rural scene. When he visited Washington in 1842, Charles Dickens complained of "spacious avenues that begin in nothing and lead nowhere."

Opposite bottom
By 1852, buildings lined both sides of Pennsylvania Avenue between the Capitol (*foreground*) and the White House. To the left of the avenue the artist shows the old Tiber Canal that bordered the Mall for many years. In 1871, the canal was filled and replaced by B Street, which later became Constitution Avenue.

By 1905 traffic on Washington's streets had already created problems, a condition that was to grow worse with time. This picture of Pennsylvania Avenue taken from the Treasury Building shows motorcars, horse-drawn vehicles, and streetcars crowding the avenue.

Opposite top
At one time during the Civil War, Union soldiers guarded the Washington end of Chain Bridge while some Confederate soldiers stood guard on the Virginia shore of the Potomac. An earlier bridge suspended by thick iron links gave the bridge its name. The present Chain Bridge was built in 1938.

Opposite bottom
Heavy rains flooded much of Washington in June, 1889. This photograph of Seventh Street was taken from Pennsylvania Avenue.

Left
The streetcar and the horse and buggy have disappeared from today's Pennsylvania Avenue, but the number of automobiles has multiplied.

Below
North Capitol Street, leading away from Capitol Hill, is another busy Washington street.

Opposite top
Because of its location on the Potomac and Anacostia rivers, bridges have played an important part in Washington's development. This picture of Arlington Memorial Bridge, one of the world's most beautiful bridges, was taken from Columbia Island with the Lincoln Memorial in the background. The bridge forms a straight line between the Lincoln Memorial and the Custis-Lee Mansion in Arlington National Cemetery, and thus symbolizes the reuniting of the North and South after the Civil War.

Opposite bottom
At Fourteenth and E streets N.W., the District Building (*left*) and the Commerce Building (*right*) form part of the base of the Federal triangle, the largest collection of government buildings in the world. Developed between 1928 and 1938, the triangle has its apex at Sixth Street.

Washington's main downtown shopping area begins at Fourteenth and F streets N.W. and then extends northwest to approximately Fifteenth and I streets and east to Seventh Street and Pennsylvania Avenue.

Some of Washington's best contemporary architecture is found in the southwest part of the city where more than five hundred acres of former slums have been cleared and replaced with apartment buildings, town houses, shopping centers, and plazas. This picture was taken from East Potomac Park.

A modern theatre-in-the-round at Sixth and M streets S.W., in the redevelopment area, is the home of the Arena Stage, Washington's well-known permanent theatrical company.

Kiosks containing city maps and other information of interest to tourists have been placed at strategic locations to help the nine million visitors who come to Washington every year.

Standing on the crest of what was once known as Jenkins Hill and is now called Capitol Hill, or simply the Hill, the gleaming white Capitol rises above the surrounding trees.

2

ON CAPITOL HILL

CAPITOL HILL IS THE CENTER OF WASHINGTON. It may not be the center geographically, because the city grew westward rather than to the east, as L'Enfant had planned, but it is the political center and the center of national and international interest. Here, on an elevation that rises to eighty-eight feet above the Potomac River, elected representatives of the people pass laws that affect not only the United States, but the entire world as well. In a white marble temple not far away, the nine justices of the Supreme Court meet to decide whether the laws are in agreement with the Constitution. And in offices on nearby streets, thousands of men and women perform the tasks, large and small, that are part of the governmental process.

Appropriately enough, Washington's street system radiates from Capitol Hill. On the city map, lines drawn from the Capitol to the four cardinal points of the compass divide the city into four sections: Northwest (N.W.), Northeast (N.E.), Southwest (S.W.), and Southeast (S.E.). North and South Capitol streets and East Capitol Street and the Mall mark the divisions. In general, the streets that run north and south are numbered, beginning at the Capitol. Also beginning at the Capitol, east and west streets are lettered through W, with J being omitted. After the lettered streets come streets with two-syllable names arranged in alphabetical order, then

three-syllable names, and finally streets named for trees and flowers. Avenues, named for the states, cut across this rectangular street pattern.

When he was working on his plans for the new Federal city, Major L'Enfant described Capitol Hill, then called Jenkins Hill, as "a pedestal waiting for a monument." The monument he proposed for the site was the Capitol. L'Enfant's plan for Jenkins Hill met with President Washington's hearty approval, and an amateur architect, Dr. William Thornton, won the ensuing competition for the best plans for a "Congress House" to be erected at the top of the hill. On September 18, 1793, George Washington, wearing a Masonic apron and wielding a silver trowel, placed the cornerstone of the new Capitol, declaring it "well and truly laid."

Once the cornerstone was laid, construction proceeded slowly for both technical and financial reasons. Dr. Thornton's plan called for an almost square central section under a low dome, with wings extending to the north and south. Several professional architects had to be dismissed because they insisted on altering this design, and finally Thornton himself agreed to finish the building with the help of James Hoban, the official government architect. A few years later, in 1796, all of the Federal funds reserved for the Capitol had been spent. The state of Maryland came to the rescue by holding a lottery and lending the proceeds to the Federal Government so that work could be resumed.

In 1800, Congress, which then numbered 32 senators and 105 representatives, moved into the new Capitol's north wing, the only part completed. President John Adams addressed the members there on November 22, 1800. Seven years later the House was meeting in its own permanent south wing, but Thornton's central section had not been completed. During this period, two wells between the north and south wings supplied thirsty congressmen with drinking water.

Construction on Capitol Hill had not progressed much further when the War of 1812 broke out, and disaster in the form of a British expeditionary force struck Washington and the unfinished Capitol. In August, 1814, the British, under Admiral Cockburn, moved overland from Chesapeake Bay to Washington, with the Capitol as one of their prime targets. Using books from the Library of Congress, then housed in the Capitol, and other inflammable material to spread the fire, Admiral Cockburn's men burned the unfinished building which Cockburn scornfully called "this harbor of Yankee democracy." The fire destroyed the wooden roofs, the interior of the House wing, part of the Senate interior, and many of the marble columns that decorated the structure.

While Congress met in temporary quarters called the "Brick Capitol," located where the Supreme Court Building now stands, architects Benjamin Latrobe and Charles Bulfinch rushed repair work on the damaged Capitol, which Latrobe described as "a most magnificent ruin." In 1819 Congress was back in the Capitol again, putting an end to suggestions that the Federal Government should move away from Washington to a safer location.

After Benjamin Latrobe resigned in 1817, Charles Bulfinch took over the job of finishing the Capitol, and in 1827 the building, as Thornton had designed it, was completed. A central section stood between the House and Senate wings; above it rose a small wooden dome.

Within a few years, Congress began to outgrow the Capitol, and in 1850 the legislators authorized extensions for both the House and Senate wings. They also ordered a new, larger dome of metal to replace the old wooden one. The members of the House moved into their new quarters in 1857; the senators moved into theirs in 1859. Work on the dome continued until 1865, although the Freedom statue was lifted into place at its top in 1863.

The Supreme Court, which had been meeting in a room on the ground floor of the Capitol, inherited the Old Senate Chamber. Some of the Court's most famous decisions were made in that chamber. The Old House Chamber remained empty until 1864 when it became the National Statuary Hall. Each state was invited to contribute two statues of honored citizens, and most did so over the years. Eventually, there was a real danger that the floor of Statuary Hall might collapse under its heavy load. Since 1930 the states have been limited to one statue apiece in Statuary Hall with a second statue placed elsewhere in the Capitol.

After the extension of the House and Senate wings, the Capitol underwent only minor changes: Steam heating was installed in 1865, elevators in 1874, and in 1881 the building was fireproofed. In 1959 and 1960, however, another major expansion took place. This time the central area of the east front was extended 32½ feet, a project that added 102 badly needed rooms to the Capitol. On the exterior of the extension, marble replaced the original sandstone. At the same time workmen removed thirty-two layers of old paint from the Capitol dome, repainted it, and cleaned the marble of the two wings.

Millions of people visit the Capitol every year. They come from all over the United States and from foreign countries to see the gleaming white building that now covers 3½ acres at the top of Capitol Hill. The doors of the Capitol are open to visitors from 9 A.M. until 5 P.M. every day, and forty-minute guided tours are available from 9 A.M. until 3:55 P.M.

Every visitor to the Capitol stops in the Rotunda to study the eight large paintings of scenes from American history and to gaze up at the huge dome rising 180 feet above the Rotunda's stone floor. The artist Constantino Brumidi made the figures in the painting that decorate the dome as much as fifteen feet tall so that they would look life-size from the floor. Brumidi did some of his work in the dome lying on his back on a scaffold.

A short corridor connects the Rotunda with Statuary Hall and the statues of the famous and the not-so-famous that line the walls of the semicircular room. Another corridor leads from Statuary Hall toward the House Chamber. When the House is in session, visitors can watch the proceedings from a gallery that provides a fine view of the legislators at work.

The oldest part of the Capitol is a hall on the Senate side of the Rotunda. After the fire in 1814, architect Latrobe decorated the hall, now called the North Small Rotunda, with a series of columns for which he designed capitals of tobacco flowers and leaves. The adjoining Old Senate Chamber, remodeled after the fire to resemble a Greek amphitheatre, housed first the Senate and then the Supreme Court. The chamber remains much as it was when the Supreme Court left it in 1935.

Like the House Chamber on the other side of the Capitol, the Senate Chamber has a gallery from which visitors can watch the proceedings on the floor below. The chamber contains no portraits, paintings, or murals (the senators outlawed all such decorations in 1884), but its damask-covered walls, cream and dark red marble pilasters, and dark mahogany desks are an impressive sight.

While most Capitol visitors stay on the main floor, some explore the ground floor as well. Here, in addition to barbershops, restaurants, and other facilities for congressmen, are statues that have overflowed from the floor above and the vaulted crypt planned for a memorial to George Washington whose tomb was to be located beneath it. That plan had to be discarded, however, when the first President's heirs decided his tomb should remain at Mount Vernon. The space beneath the crypt now holds the velvet-draped catafalque used when national heroes lie in state in the Rotunda. A piece of white marble in the crypt floor marks the exact center of the Capitol.

The Capitol is surrounded by 120 acres of landscaped grounds containing a variety of trees and shrubs. The green and parklike grounds are bordered by Constitution Avenue on the north, by Independence Avenue on the south, and First Street N.W. and S.W. on the west. On the east the grounds slope away to First Street N.E. and S.E. and the Library of Congress, one of the world's great libraries.

Established in 1800 with an appropriation of $5,000 "for the purchase of such books as may be necessary for the use of Congress at . . . Washington, and for fitting up a suitable apartment for containing them," the Library occupied rooms in the Capitol until 1897. Like the rest of the Capitol, it was severely damaged in the 1814 fire. Because most of its own book collection was destroyed, Congress in 1815 purchased Thomas Jefferson's 6,487-volume collection as the basis for a new library.

During its years in the Capitol, the Library of Congress grew larger and larger, quickly filling any additional space that could be found for it. Finally, in 1886, Congress appropriated $500,000 to start the construction of a new library building; it was completed eleven years later at a cost of $6,500,000.

The Library of Congress is one of the most lavishly decorated buildings in Washington. Inside and out it displays a profusion of sculpture and other ornamentation. In addition, the interior contains elaborate marble stairways, paired Corinthian columns supporting decorated vaulted ceilings, and numerous murals and mosaics. In this building and the plainer five-story annex behind it, the Library of Congress maintains collections that total more than forty-four million items, which makes it the largest library in the world. In addition to books, the Library of Congress handles manuscripts, maps, photographs, prints and drawings, musical works, motion pictures, microfilms, newspapers, periodicals, and many other kinds of materials.

Although only congressmen and a limited number of other persons can withdraw books from the Library of Congress, the library's reading rooms are open to anyone over high-school age. Those who wish to observe rather than to read can do so from a gallery overlooking the famous octagonal reading room in the main building. The gallery provides a fine view of the reading room below and of the many statues, columns, carvings, and stained glass windows that decorate it.

In the halls outside the main reading room and in other areas the Library displays its greatest treasures. Some of them, like the Gutenberg Bible and the rough draft of the Declaration of Independence, are on permanent display. Other exhibits are changed periodically.

The Library of Congress is open from 9 A.M. until 10 P.M. on weekdays, from 9 A.M. until 6 P.M. on Saturdays, and from 2 P.M. until 6 P.M. on

Sundays. Thirty-minute conducted tours are available on weekdays between 9:15 A.M. and 4 P.M.

Another famous library occupies the same Capitol Hill block as the Library of Congress annex, but the Folger Shakespeare Library is privately endowed, rather than government owned. It specializes in Shakespeareana and materials in English dealing with the sixteenth and seventeenth centuries.

In designing the library building, architect Paul Philippe Crét successfully adapted a modern exterior to the classic and Renaissance styles of the library's neighbors on Capitol Hill. The interior of the library is Elizabethan to provide a suitable background for the many items from that period on display. The oak-paneled Exhibition Hall reproduces a great hall in an Elizabethan palace, the reading room is another Elizabethan hall, and in the east wing an Elizabethan theatre reproduces the inn-courtyard theatres of seventeenth-century England.

Across East Capitol Street from the Library of Congress and the Folger Shakespeare Library, the Supreme Court Building draws its inspiration from the marble temples of Greece. Considered by many to be one of the finest buildings in the United States, it has been the home of the Supreme Court since it moved from the Capitol in 1935.

The Supreme Court meets in a large, beautifully decorated chamber where each of the nine justices has an assigned chair at the bench which occupies a dais at one end of the room. When the court is in session from October to June each year, visitors are admitted to the courtroom as seats become available. But even when the court is not in session, a visit is well worthwhile. Guides lead groups through the building, making stops at the courtroom, the imposing main hall lined with Doric columns, the elegant spiral staircases that wind through five floors, and other points of interest. The sections of the building where the justices and their staffs work are not open to the public.

On streets adjacent to the Capitol grounds, five large buildings provide office space for members of the Senate and the House and their assistants. Senators have accommodations in the Old and New Senate Office buildings located north of the Supreme Court Building and northeast of the Capitol. Representatives have their offices in the Cannon, Longworth, and Rayburn buildings (named for former

Speakers of the House) located across Independence Avenue from the Capitol. In addition to offices, the five buildings have committee rooms where public hearings are held and various facilities, such as gymnasiums and dining rooms, for the use of congressmen. A subway system, open to the public, connects the House and Senate office buildings with the Capitol.

Across Independence Avenue from the Rayburn Building, at the southwestern edge of the Capitol grounds, is the large greenhouse known as the Botanic Garden. Operated by Congress through its Joint Committee on the Library of Congress and supervised by the Architect of the Capitol, the Botanic Garden cultivates and displays both native and foreign plants for the benefit of students and scientists and for those who merely like to observe beautiful and unusual botanical specimens.

Congress took the first step toward the establishment of what was to become the Botanic Garden in 1842 when it provided accommodations for the botanical specimens collected in the South Seas by the United States Exploring Expedition of 1838–1842. The Botanic Garden, which moved to its present quarters in 1934, now has over ten thousand species and varieties of plants.

Although Union Station, on the northeastern boundary of Capitol Hill, no longer serves as the major gateway to Washington, it remains one of the city's most distinguished structures. As the first building constructed after the McMillan Commission presented its plan for a more beautiful Washington, Union Station was carefully designed to provide an appropriate introduction to the nation's Capital and its Roman classic style influenced Washington architecture for many years.

At one time over two hundred trains belonging to seven railroads used Union Station's twenty upper-level and twelve lower-level tracks each day. A 760-foot-long concourse providing access to the trains was especially designed to handle huge crowds attending special Washington events such as Presidential inaugurations.

After World War II, declining railway traffic left Union Station almost empty, and serious consideration was given to tearing it down, much to the dismay of the country's architects who admired the building. Union Station was saved, however, when

Congress passed a law converting it into a National Visitor Center, and in that capacity it will continue to serve visitors to the nation's Capital.

Although it is several blocks away, the Congressional Cemetery in southeast Washington was closely connected with Capitol Hill during much of the nineteenth century, when it served as the semi-official burying ground for members of Congress and other public officials. What became the Congressional Cemetery was actually a part of the Christ Church burial ground which Congress reserved by giving financial assistance to the church in 1816. Government officials had been buried there prior to 1816, however.

William Thornton, the man who designed the Capitol, was buried in Congressional Cemetery as was Elbridge Gerry, one of the signers of the Declaration of Independence, and Push-Ma-Ta-Ha, an Indian chief who died in Washington in 1825 while negotiating a treaty with the United States Government. President Zachary Taylor and Dolley Madison, the wife of the fourth President of the United States, were temporarily interred there.

When the coming of the railroads made it possible for most government officials to be buried in their home states, the use of Congressional Cemetery declined, although for many years cenotaphs were placed there for senators and representatives who died in office, whether they were buried in the cemetery or elsewhere. In presenting a motion in 1877 that the practice be abolished, Senator Hoar of Massachusetts described the cenotaphs as being so ugly that the prospect of being interred beneath one added a new terror to death.

Today, quiet Congressional Cemetery with its cenotaphs and old graves recalls a Capitol Hill of another era.

With the exception of President William Howard Taft, every President since Andrew Jackson has been inaugurated on the steps of the east front of the Capitol. Because of inclement weather, President Taft's inauguration was held in the Senate Chamber.

This nighttime photograph of the Capitol's west front shows the floodlighted central section and the two original wings.

Opposite, top right
St. Peter's Church in Rome provided the model for the cap of the Capitol dome. The thirteen fluted Corinthian columns surmounting the cap represent the first thirteen states.

Opposite, top left
A closeup of the 19½-foot, 14,985-pound bronze statue of Freedom that crowns the Capitol dome shows her to be holding a sword in one hand and a shield and a wreath in the other. The statue, the work of the American sculptor, Thomas Crawford, was hoisted into place on December 2, 1963.

Opposite bottom
Only the Senate wing had been completed when Congress met in the Capitol for the first time on November 21, 1800.

By 1814, the Capitol had two stone wings joined by a wooden arcade, or walk-way. This drawing shows Pennsylvania Avenue in the foreground.

Opposite top
A wooden dome crowned the Capitol after 1827. This is the west front with Pennsylvania Avenue in the foreground.

A VIEW OF THE CAPITOL OF THE UNITED STATES
after the Conflagration of the 24th August 1814.

A contemporary engraving shows the damage suffered by the Capitol, when the British Expeditionary force set it afire on August 24, 1814.

An 1848 lithograph shows the Senate in session. This is the room in which the Supreme Court met between 1860 and 1935. Since 1935, it has been used for occasional committee hearings and receptions.

In 1848, the House of Representatives was still meeting in the chamber that later became the National Statuary Hall.

At a well-attended ceremony on July 4, 1851, President Millard Fillmore laid the cornerstone for the House extension to the Capitol. It was completed in 1857; a Senate extension was finished in 1859.

LAYING OF THE CORNER STONE AT THE CAPITOL.

Work on the Capitol continued during the Civil War. This photograph was probably taken in 1862.

Plan of the Capitol's main floor.

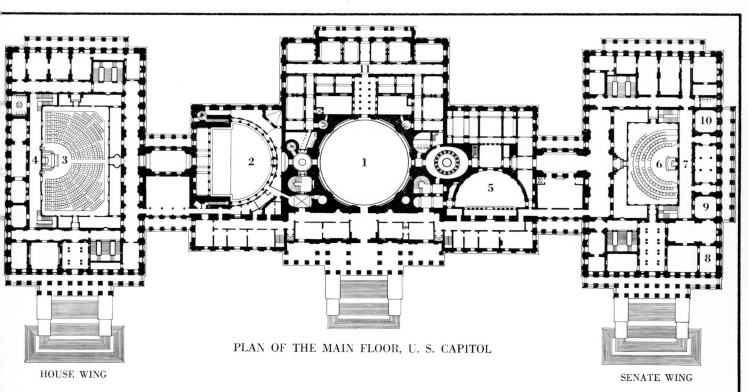

PLAN OF THE MAIN FLOOR, U. S. CAPITOL

HOUSE WING

SENATE WING

. Great Rotunda
. Statuary Hall
. House of Representatives

4. Speaker's Lobby
5. Former Supreme Court
   Chamber

6. Senate Chamber
7. Senate Lobby
8. Majority Leader's Room

9. Vice President's Room
10. President's Room
11. Former Library of Congress

The Senate has conducted its business in this chamber since 1859. The one hundred mahogany desks are assigned by seniority with Republicans on the left of the Vice President, who serves as the Senate's presiding officer, and Democrats on the right.

The House Chamber, with seats for 435 representatives, is one of the largest legislative chambers in the world. Joint meetings and sessions of Congress are held here. Except on guided tours, visitors to both the House and Senate galleries need a pass obtainable from members of the House or Senate.

The great mace of the United States (*left*) stands beside the Speaker's desk when the House is in regular session. Its removal to a lower pedestal means that the House is acting as a Committee of the Whole on the State of the Union with fewer members needed to make a quorum. The present mace, a bundle of ebony rods topped by a silver globe and eagle, replaces the original mace destroyed when the Capitol burned in 1814.

Although it is seldom used now, Presidents once came to the ornate President's Room during the last hours of their administrations to sign bills into law. The room was decorated by the Italian artist Constantino Brumidi. He worked on various Capitol rooms and halls from 1855 until his death in 1880.

The Rotunda, a large circular hall that measures one hundred feet across, is the heart of the Capitol. It displays some of the Capitol's best painting and sculpture beneath a huge dome decorated by Brumidi. The nation's honored dead have lain in state in the Rotunda while mourning citizens filed by their black-draped biers.

This marble statue of Ethan Allen was one of the first to be displayed in Statuary Hall. Allen, from Vermont, was a Revolutionary War soldier and an author.

Architect Benjamin Latrobe designed his famous tobacco-leaf capitals for columns in the North Small Rotunda. Latrobe was in charge of Capitol construction from 1803 until 1817.

In the crypt under the Rotunda, three female heads set on a large block of marble honor pioneer suffragettes Lucretia Mott, Elizabeth Cady, and Susan B. Anthony. The statue has been nicknamed "Ladies in a Bathtub."

Each state has the privilege of placing one statue of an outstanding, deceased citizen in Statuary Hall and another in the Hall of Columns or elsewhere in the Capitol. Statuary Hall is one of the most handsome rooms in the Capitol, but its statues, executed in a number of styles and materials, vary in quality.

Nondenominational and severely simple in design, the Capitol Prayer Room provides a quiet place for congressional meditation and prayer. A kneeling figure of George Washington decorates the stained glass window above the altar.

Opposite top
Twenty-seven bells hang in the upper part of the Robert A. Taft Memorial. The bells, the largest of which weighs seven tons, toll the hours and the quarter hours.

Opposite bottom
On the northwestern slope of the Capitol grounds a one-hundred-foot-high bell tower commemorates the late Senator Robert A. Taft of Ohio.

On the north side of the Capitol grounds the Spring Grotto offers a shady retreat. The grotto was designed by Frederick Law Olmstead, who landscaped the grounds during the last half of the nineteenth century. Once fed by a spring, the grotto now flows with city water.

A close view of the Library of Congress reveals its ornate architectural style, inspired in part by the Paris Opera House.

This picture was taken in 1893, when the Library of Congress was under construction. The east front of the Capitol can be seen at the right.

A representation of the Flame of Knowledge tops the intricately sculptured dome of the Library of Congress.

The gilded inner shell of the Library of Congress dome rises to a height of 125 feet above the main reading room.

Paired Corinthian columns of white Italian marble surround the cases in which the Library of Congress displays choice items from its vast collections.

Elaborate marble stairways lead to the lavishly decorated galleries around the Great Hall of the Library of Congress.

Some of Washington's most ornate ceilings are in the Library of Congress. This detail is from a second-floor ceiling.

In the main reading room of the Library of Congress, mahogany desks are arranged in circles around the central issue desk. The reading room can be viewed from the visitors' gallery in the mezzanine of the second floor.

Beautifully decorated bronze doors guard the entrance to the rare book room on the library's second floor. The door's six panels carry the names or devices of famous printers and book designers.

This representation of "History" is one of the many statues that decorate the main reading room.

The Library of Congress has the only perfect copy of a Gutenberg Bible on vellum in the United States. It is on permanent display in the Great Hall.

Many of the library's rare books are works of art. This manuscript was copied and decorated by a fifteenth-century scribe.

The congressional reading room on the first floor of the main building is one of the library's fourteen special reading rooms. It is used by members of Congress and their staff assistants.

Located east of the main building across Second Street S.E., the white marble Library of Congress annex was designed to provide shelf space for ten million books. It opened in 1939. A third library building, a memorial to President James Madison, will be ready for occupancy early in the 1970's. It will be located south of the main building.

The Thomas Jefferson Room on the fifth floor of the annex is the library's second general reading room. The famous Thomas Jefferson murals by Ezra Winter decorate its upper panels.

The Library of Congress maintains two general card catalogs, one in the main reading room and one adjacent to the Thomas Jefferson Room (*illustrated here*). The special reading rooms have their own catalogs.

THE EARTH BELONGS ALWAYS TO THE LIVING GENERATION · THEY MAY MANAGE IT THEN AND WHAT PROCEEDS FROM IT AS THEY PLEASE DURING THEIR USUFRUCT · THEY ARE MASTERS TOO OF THEIR OWN PERSONS AND CONSEQUENTLY MAY GOVERN THEM AS THEY PLEASE.

One of the four panels that make up the Thomas Jefferson murals is painted around the clock on the reading room's south wall. It contains a quotation from the third President's writings and groups of figures from his time against a background of ancient architecture.

40

Library of Congress displays are not devoted exclusively to books. The library's three Stradivari violins along with a viola and a cello, also by the Italian master, can be seen in a specially ventilated case in the library's Whittall Pavilion. Musicians who perform at the library's chamber music concerts in Coolidge Auditorium use the instruments.

Neptune, the ancient Roman god of the sea, is the central figure in the large fountain in front of the main entrance to the Library of Congress. Neptune is flanked by two nymphs riding sea horses.

The handsome white marble Folger Shakespeare Library at 201 East Capitol Street S.E. is a neighbor of the Library of Congress on Capitol Hill. Founded and endowed by Henry Clay Folger and administered by Amherst College, the Folger Shakespeare Library has the largest collection of Shakespeare materials in the world and an outstanding collection of works about the sixteenth and seventeenth centuries.

Opposite
Located in the central section of the building, the reading room of the Folger Shakespeare Library was designed to resemble an English great hall. All of the library's rooms are decorated in the style of seventeenth-century England.

One of the many attractions of the Folger Library is an Elizabethan theatre in the east wing. While it does not copy a particular theatre, it reproduces a typical playhouse in which Shakespeare's plays may have been presented. The library is open daily, except Sunday, from 10 A.M. until 4:30 P.M. (The reading room opens at 9 A.M.)

Opposite top
The majestic white marble Supreme Court Building faces the Capitol across a wide plaza. One of the finest examples of classic architecture in Washington, it was completed in 1935. The building is open from 9 A.M. until 4:30 P.M. on weekdays and from 9 A.M. until noon on Saturdays. There are free tours when the court is not in session.

Opposite center
The Cannon Building, New Jersey and Independence avenues S.E., seen here, and its almost identical twin, the Old Senate Office Building at First and B streets N.E., were erected in the first decade of the twentieth century to provide badly needed office space for members of the House and Senate.

Opposite bottom
After the reapportionment that followed the 1910 census increased its membership, the House of Representatives needed a second office building. The result was the Longworth Building, located directly across the street from the Cannon Building.

Its price tag of $98.2 million makes the Rayburn Building (*above*) the most expensive office building in the world. In addition to offices for 169 congressmen, it contains hearing rooms, two gymnasiums, a sixty- by twenty-foot swimming pool, and parking space for sixteen hundred cars in an underground garage. The building is located at South Capitol Street and Independence Avenue S.W.

A bearded figure representing the majesty of law guards one of the entrances to the Rayburn Building.

The New Senate Office Building at First Street and Constitution Avenue N.E. is one of the two buildings on Capitol Hill in which members of the Senate have offices.

Below
The Government Printing Office is equipped with these Linotype machines and a variety of other equipment for printing and binding government publications. When Congress is in session, the printing office turns out a word-by-word account of each day's proceedings, called the Congressional Record, and delivers a copy to each congressman's desk by 8 o'clock the next morning.

These buildings on North Capitol Street between G and H streets house what may be the largest printing plant in the world, the United States Government Printing Office. As the government's official printer, it turns out a vast array of publications many of which can be purchased in the building or by mail.

Architect Daniel H. Burnham borrowed many of Union Station's details from ancient Rome including the three arches at the front of the building. Its large waiting room is based on the central hall in the Baths of Diocletian. A Washington landmark since it opened in 1907, the station covers twenty-five acres.

Opposite top
Surrounded by tropical foliage, a pair of visitors to the conservatory of the United States Botanic Garden inspects an array of potted plants. The Botanic Garden, on Maryland Avenue between First and Second streets S.W., contains many varieties of palms, ferns, cacti, orchids, and other tropical and subtropical plants. There are several special displays each year. The Botanic Garden is open daily, except Saturday, from 9 A.M. until 4 P.M. The Saturday hours are 9 A.M. until noon.

Opposite, bottom left
Frederic Auguste Bartholdi, sculptor of the Statue of Liberty, designed the fountain at Second and B streets S.W., near the Botanic Garden.

Opposite, bottom right
This is a closeup of the top of the Bartholdi fountain, considered by many to be Washington's most graceful fountain.

Figures representing the old and the new world decorate the Columbus Memorial Fountain in the Union Station Plaza.

From the fountains and statues of the Union Station Plaza it is only a half mile to the Capitol. This approach offers a good view of the Capitol's east front.

Opposite top
The Congressional Cemetery, at Eighteenth and E streets S.E., was once the semiofficial burying ground for members of Congress and other public officials.

Opposite bottom
Between 1838 and 1877, eighty-five cenotaphs like those in the foreground were erected in Congressional Cemetery to honor senators and representatives who died in office, although many of them were buried in their home states. The cenotaph in the left foreground carries the name of John C. Calhoun; the one on the right was erected in memory of Henry Clay. Neither man was buried in Congressional Cemetery.

A mile west of the Capitol the White House presents its imposing north front to Pennsylvania Avenue. A curving drive leads to the Executive Mansion's official entrance.

3

THE PRESIDENT'S HOUSE

EVERY ONE OF OUR PRESIDENTS EXCEPT GEORGE WASHINGTON has lived in the White House, but the first President did help to choose its location. In those days the site of the future White House, or President's House, as it was called then, was a stretch of rough and barren land that terminated in the swamps that bordered the Potomac River. It did offer a fine view of the river, however, a view that has since been cut off.

At the same time that the commissioners of the Federal city sponsored a contest for the design of the Capitol, they held a second competition for a President's House. Thomas Jefferson, then serving as George Washington's Secretary of State, submitted an entry, as did several other amateur and professional architects. The winning design was the work of James Hoban, an Irish architect then a resident of Charleston, South Carolina. His plan for the President's House called for a two-story building in the popular Georgian style with a large American eagle decorating the pediment in the front.

Although work on the President's House began immediately, it was still unfinished when the Government moved to Washington in 1800. Construction had progressed far enough, however, to permit President John Adams to move in on November 1, 1800. Shortly thereafter he wrote: "I pray Heaven to bestow the best of Blessings on this House and all that shall hereafter inhabit it." Many years later President

Franklin D. Roosevelt had Adams' words carved on the mantel in the State Dining Room.

During the winter that she spent in the President's House, First Lady Abigail Adams struggled to make the unfinished building livable. She wrote to her daughter: "We have not the least fence, yard or other convenience, without, and the great unfinished audience room [the East Room] I make a drying-room of, to hang up the clothes in. The principal stairs are not up, and will not be this winter."

The second resident of the White House, widower Thomas Jefferson, described it as "big enough for two emperors, one Pope and the Grand Lama." Nevertheless, he asked architect Benjamin Latrobe to design terraces and pavilions for the east and west sides of the building, and a north and a south portico. The low terrace-pavilions were completed in 1807, while Jefferson still lived in the White House; the porticoes were added later.

The White House, sparsely furnished when the Adamses lived there, had become an elegant residence by the time James Madison succeeded President Jefferson in 1809. All was lost, however, when the British burned the Executive Mansion in 1814. Only a heavy rain saved the shell of the building from total destruction.

When President James Monroe moved into the rebuilt White House in 1817, it was once again sparsely furnished, although architect James Hoban had successfully restored the building according to his original plans. Monroe brought some of his own furniture to the White House and ordered $15,567.43 worth of elegant new furniture from France. Records on the subject are sketchy, but it may have been at this time that the exterior of the building was painted white to cover the marks left by the fire.

Throughout its long history, the White House has undergone major remodeling only a few times, but there have been numerous changes in its furnishings and many minor alterations in its structure. In the years after the rebuilding necessitated by the fire, the south and north porticoes were added, in 1824 and 1829 respectively. Gas lighting came to the White House in 1848 during James Polk's Presidency. City water was piped into the building in 1853, but bathrooms were not added until 1878 when President Rutherford B. Hayes occupied the Executive Mansion. Benjamin Harrison was the first President to enjoy electricity in the White House. He also had a one-line telephone. Congress, however, refused to act on Mrs. Harrison's plan for greatly enlarging the mansion.

In spite of Congress' stand on enlarging the White House, it was generally agreed that something should be done to give the First Family more living space. The second floor, for example, had developed into a crowded jumble of private family rooms and public offices. In 1901 the crowding became worse when President Theodore Roosevelt, who had six children, moved into the White House.

An extensive White House remodeling project, under the direction of the architectural firm of Mc-Kim, Mead and White, began in 1902. The architects removed the greenhouses that had spread over the west lawn to expose the pavilion that Thomas Jefferson built there in 1807. They added a windowed gallery to that pavilion and to the one on the east side of the White House, and erected a small office building at the end of the west gallery.

Inside the White House all of the main rooms underwent renovation and redecoration as the often ornate furniture and ornamentation installed over the years by various First Families were removed and replaced by a more simple style. For White House hostesses, one important change was the removal of a stairway to make the State Dining Room bigger. At large dinners it had been necessary to serve some guests in an adjoining hall or in the East Room.

In 1927, when the White House needed reroofing, the new roof was raised enough to turn the former attic into a third floor. Twenty years later, while President Harry Truman occupied the White House, vibrating floors were traced to the 1927 roof and the third story which had been laid on old walls too weak to bear the added weight. The structural strength of the building had also been weakened by other changes made over the years, with the result that the White House was no longer safe to live in.

As an alternative to tearing the building down, architects decided that the entire inner structure could be removed and replaced with a steel framework. They proceeded to do this between 1949 and 1952, while President Truman and his family lived at Blair House, across Pennsylvania Avenue from the White House. When the project was finished and the original paneling, trim, and decorations had been reinstated, the Trumans moved back into the White House. President Truman had hoped to refurnish the Executive Mansion with fine antiques and various items that were associated with past Presidents. Budgetary limitations made this impossible, however, and the Trumans decided to use some of the furniture purchased for the White House in 1902 augmented by good reproductions of antiques.

President Truman's plans for refurnishing the White House continued a tradition that began in 1889, when Mrs. Benjamin Harrison collected china that had been used in the Executive Mansion by former First Families. Since then, Presidential wives, and sometimes Presidents, have taken an active interest in acquiring for the White House furniture and other items once used there.

During the Kennedy Administration a fine arts committee for the White House, organized by Mrs. John F. Kennedy, developed an overall plan for decorating and furnishing the Executive Mansion and acquired many of the items now in use or displayed there. President Lyndon B. Johnson subsequently established a committee for the preservation of the White House to insure that its historic furnishings would be cared for. As a result of these actions and the steps taken by past administrations, the White House has become a living memorial to the country's past and a fitting symbol of the Presidency.

Just as the White House has changed over the

years, its grounds, officially the President's Park, have changed too. Originally the grounds, then called the President's Square, included both Lafayette Square and the Ellipse, about eighty acres in all. The Ellipse, a round park south of the White House, is still considered a part of the President's Park.

When President John Adams moved into the White House in 1800, the grounds were unimproved and partly occupied by shacks in which the men working on the White House lived. During his term of office, which began in 1825, President John Quincy Adams saw to it that the grounds were graded and fenced and he spent many hours working in the White House flower gardens. President Martin Van Buren added fountains, stone walls, iron railings, stables, and gardens planted with native and exotic plants. In 1851 the grounds were formally laid out by Andrew Jackson Downing, a noted landscape designer. Some of his work can still be seen, although, like the White House itself, the grounds have reflected the tastes of succeeding Presidents.

A fence encloses the eighteen acres of the President's Park immediately surrounding the White House. This area is normally not open to the public, but on Easter Monday the children of Washington are invited to the south lawn for the traditional egg-rolling. Adults must be accompanied by a child in order to be admitted. The south lawn is also used for outdoor ceremonies and receptions, and the Presidential helicopters land there. The more formal north lawn is an expanse of green leading to Pennsylvania Avenue. Its central fountain is surrounded by flower beds. Tall trees shade the drive that curves up to the main entrance of the White House.

From the White House the President can look out across the north lawn and Pennsylvania Avenue to Lafayette Square, which George Washington proposed for a public park as early as 1791. The two-block area was included in the original President's Square and at one time contained a racetrack, a marketplace, and a parade ground. During most of the nineteenth century, however, it was a pleasant, informal park surrounded by some of Washington's most prestigious residences.

Commodore Stephen Decatur built the oldest house on the square in 1818, when he returned from the Barbary Coast campaigns against the pirates. After he was killed in a duel a few years later, a succession of famous men lived in Decatur House, including Martin Van Buren, who later became the eighth President of the United States. The National Trust for Historic Preservation now owns the house and operates it as a museum.

The President's Guest House faces Pennsylvania Avenue rather than Lafayette Square, but it is usually considered to be one of the square's historic houses. The Guest House is actually two houses— Blair House at 1651 Pennsylvania Avenue and the adjoining Blair-Lee House, built for a Blair daughter at 1653 Pennsylvania Avenue.

Blair House, which dates back to 1824, was purchased in 1836 by Francis Preston Blair, from whom it takes its name. Presidents and other important officials were frequent visitors to Blair House, and at the beginning of the Civil War Robert E. Lee was offered the command of the Union Army there, which he declined.

The United States Government acquired the Blair-Lee House in 1941 and Blair House in 1942. Since then many distinguished visitors from other countries have been entertained in the President's Guest House.

A plaque at the front entrance of Blair House commemorates a White House guard who was killed on November 1, 1950, by two men who tried to force their way into the house to assassinate President Truman, then living at Blair House during the renovation of the Executive Mansion.

Although most of Lafayette Square's old houses have disappeared, it remains popular with both Washingtonians and tourists. From the square they can catch a glimpse of the White House and, occasionally, of important visitors coming or going. But most of all, in Lafayette Square they can enjoy an attractive park in the midst of the Capital city's bustle.

As a park, Lafayette Square has been kept informal in design, with winding asphalt paths, many varieties of trees and shrubs, and colorful beds of flowers. A statue commemorating a foreign patriot who fought in the American Revolution stands in each of its four corners with the statue of the Marquis de Lafayette, for whom the square was named, occupying the southeast corner. In the center of the square, Andrew Jackson, the seventh President of the United States, memorialized with a bronze equestrian statue, tips his hat to White House visitors.

Opposite top
Architect Benjamin Latrobe made this drawing for President Thomas Jefferson. It shows the north and south porticoes that Latrobe proposed adding to the White House. Work on the south portico was completed in 1824; the north portico was finished in 1829.

Opposite bottom
An 1848 lithograph shows the graceful Ionic columns of Latrobe's north portico. The iron fence that runs along Pennsylvania Avenue was installed in 1833 and replaced in 1902.

Underneath the dazzling white paint that covers the White House are walls of gray Virginia sandstone. This is the south façade.

View of the East front of the Presidents House, with the addition of the North & South Porticos.

For many years, the President's New Year's Day reception was a popular White House social event. This photograph was taken at the north entrance during President Grover Cleveland's reception on New Year's Day, 1891.

Opposite top
This photograph was taken in 1861, the year Abraham Lincoln moved into the White House. The statue of Thomas Jefferson that stood in front of the Executive Mansion in Lincoln's day was moved to the Capitol in 1874. It is now in the Capitol Rotunda.

3–6
Opposite bottom
Extensive greenhouses once occupied the area west of the White House. During Theodore Roosevelt's administration they were replaced by an executive office wing.

Walls covered with watered moss-green silk and curtains of the same material give the Green Room its name. It is used for informal receptions.

Opposite top
The state rooms on the first floor of the White House are approached through the spacious entrance hall. The hall has marble floors and walls, and is lighted by a large glass lantern.

Opposite bottom
The white and gold East Room, the largest room in the White House, is used for state receptions and balls. It has also been the scene of several White House weddings and funerals.

In 1893 cut-velvet upholstery covered the chairs and sofas of the Blue Room. The room was decorated in much the same style in 1886 when President Grover Cleveland was married to Frances Folsom there, in the only Presidential marriage to take place in the White House.

Opposite top
Guests at small White House receptions gather in the Red Room. Its walls are covered with magenta-red silk. Draperies and upholstery are in a matching fabric.

Opposite bottom
Portraits of our first seven Presidents decorate the walls of the Blue Room, where the Chief Executive receives his guests prior to state dinners and receptions. A draped valance of blue encircles the elliptical-shaped room. Curtains and window valances are also blue.

Large White House dinners are held in the State Dining Room. Its oak-paneled walls are painted white. Gold-colored draperies at the windows complement a large gilded chandelier and gilded wall sconces.

Below
The President's oval-shaped office is located in the Executive Mansion's west wing. French doors open onto a colonnade and the White House rose garden.

Once the President's Cabinet Room, the Treaty Room on the second floor of the White House received its present name from the many treaties signed there. The room has been restored with some of its original furniture.

The Lincoln Bedroom adjoining the Treaty Room contains the eight-foot bed used by the Civil War President.

The shelves of the White House library hold books that were especially selected to represent American thought and tradition. The ground-floor room is decorated in the style of the early nineteenth century.

Wallpaper featuring American scenes from the early 1800's decorates the oval Diplomatic Reception Room. Guests at state functions enter the White House by way of this ground-floor room.

Decatur House at 748 Jackson Place N.W., built in 1818 and the first private residence on Lafayette Square, is now open to the public daily from noon until 5 P.M.

Historic Decatur House has been restored according to architect Benjamin Latrobe's original plans for it. This is the drawing room on the second floor.

Two fine old Washington houses, the Blair and Blair-Lee houses at 1651–1653 Pennsylvania Avenue, just off Lafayette Square, have served as the President's guest houses since 1942. Heads of state and other dignitaries stay there during their visits to Washington.

In the southeast corner of Lafayette Square, a statue of the Marquis de Lafayette, who fought with the Continental Army during the Revolutionary War, carries the inscription: "To General Lafayette and His Compatriots, 1777–1783."

From the center of Lafayette Square Andrew Jackson, commemorated by a bronze statue cast from cannon that he captured during the War of 1812, looks toward the White House where he lived between 1829 and 1837 as the seventh President of the United States.

4

MEMORIALS TO OUR PRESIDENTS

MEMORIALS ABOUND IN WASHINGTON. There are memorials to statesmen, military heroes, scientists, and poets, to mention only a few. Of them all, the most impressive by far are the memorials that honor Presidents of the United States.

Perhaps the best known of the Capital's memorials is the Washington National Monument, a towering, 555-foot marble shaft honoring our first President. It is a monument that took shape slowly after many years of discussion followed by more years of off-again, on-again construction.

The first proposals for expressing the new nation's gratitude to George Washington were made during his lifetime. One of them called for an equestrian statue, an idea that pleased the first President, and with his city planner, L'Enfant, he chose a site for it on the Mall. Lack of funds made it necessary to postpone the commissioning of the statue, however, and Washington died before anything further was done. The next proposal for honoring the first President involved the construction of a mausoleum under the Capital Rotunda, but Washington's heirs decided his tomb should remain at Mount Vernon. Congressional attention then turned once again to a statue. The result was the controversial toga-clad statue of Washington executed by Horatio Green-

ough, now on view in the Smithsonian Institution's Museum of History and Technology.

While Greenough was working on his statue, a group of citizens, dissatisfied with the actions of Congress, organized the Washington National Monument Society to raise funds for a "great National Monument to the memory of Washington at the seat of the Federal Government." All Americans were asked to contribute, and by 1847 seventy thousand dollars had been collected. Although that sum was far short of the estimated million dollars that would be needed, the cornerstone for a six-hundred-foot obelisk was laid on July 4, 1848, with the silver trowel wielded by George Washington at the laying of the Capitol cornerstone used again on this occasion.

The shortage of funds made it necessary for the National Monument Society to discard all but the essentials of architect-engineer Robert Mills's design for an elaborate obelisk-monument, and continuing difficulties aggravated by the impending Civil War finally brought construction to a complete halt. For twenty-two years the monument stood at 153 feet. A change in the color of the monument's marble at this level still marks the point at which work was suspended. Although the marble used above 153

Opposite
The highest structure in the nation's Capital commemorates the first President of the United States. In the first row of buildings behind the 555-foot Washington Monument are from left: the Department of Labor, the Interstate Commerce Commission, and the Internal Revenue Service.

feet came from the same vein as the older marble, it had weathered to a different shade.

Work on the Washington Monument resumed in 1880, with Federal funds and with the Engineer Corps of the War Department in charge, and proceeded without further delay to the laying of the capstone on December 6, 1884. The monument was opened to the public in 1888. Since then millions of Americans have visited it at a rate that now has reached approximately two million each year. The more hardy climb the 898 steps to the observation platform at the top; the others make the ascent in one minute by elevator. The climbers can examine the 190 memorial blocks set in the stairway walls, which the elevator riders miss, but once at the top, both groups enjoy an unparalleled view of Washington.

Thomas Jefferson's stately memorial was dedicated on April 13, 1943, the two hundredth anniversary of his birth. Its location on the south shore of the Tidal Basin completes a crosslike plan for the location of Washington's important structures in which the Capitol, the Washington Monument, and the Lincoln Memorial form the east-west axis, with the White House, the Washington Monument again, and the Jefferson Memorial forming the north-south axis. Two of these sites, the Capitol and the White House, along with the Mall, were part of L'Enfant's original plan for Washington.

As in the case of the Jefferson Memorial, the Lincoln Memorial site was deliberately chosen to carry out the overall plan for the location of the Capital's important buildings and monuments. Construction of the memorial began in 1914, almost a half century after Lincoln's death during which a number of attempts to secure a memorial for the Civil War President ended in failure. The final result, however, was a memorial worthy of one of the nation's greatest heroes.

Although its design is similar to that of the Parthenon, the temple to the goddess Athena in Athens, Greece, the Lincoln Memorial actually symbolizes the union of the states. Its thirty-six columns represent the states in the Union at the time of Lincoln's death. Their names are listed on a frieze above the colonnade, and the forty-eight states comprising the Union at the time the memorial was built are listed above the frieze.

The interior of the memorial with its striking figure of Lincoln seated in a curule chair and its walls inscribed with his Second Inaugural and Gettysburg addresses is equally impressive. Very few of the many thousands who visit it each year fail to be moved by the brooding figure of Lincoln in his temple-like memorial.

The Lincoln Memorial is administered by the National Park Service, as are the Washington Monument and the Jefferson Memorial. The Park Service also administers three other Washington memorials to the Civil War President: Lincoln Park with its Emancipation Statue; Ford's Theatre at 511 Tenth Street N.W., where Lincoln was shot while watching a performance of *Our American Cousin,* and the house where Lincoln died, across the street from the theatre. The latter has been equipped with furnishings of the Lincoln era, and Ford's Theatre has recently been restored to the appearance it had when Lincoln was a patron. Plays are once again presented at the theatre, making Ford's a living memorial to the great Civil War President.

Theodore Roosevelt has an island in the Potomac River as his memorial. Roosevelt Island is a memorial that would have pleased the twenty-sixth President, who was an ardent conservationist, for the island is maintained as a wilderness area with many different kinds of plant and animal life. A bridge that arches above the southern tip of the island as it connects Washington with Arlington, Virginia, also bears Roosevelt's name.

Washington's newest Presidential memorial is the John F. Kennedy Center for the Performing Arts, with facilities for opera, drama, concerts, and cinema in one large building designed by architect Edward Durell Stone. What was to become "the sole national memorial" to the assassinated thirty-fifth President began in 1958 as a plan to establish a national cultural center in Washington. The act of Congress authorizing the center stipulated that it was to be a bureau of the Smithsonian Institution under the direction of a special board of trustees, and that money for its construction was to be raised by voluntary contributions. Of the $75 million needed, only a little more than a million dollars had been raised when President Kennedy entered the White House in January, 1961. Hoping to save the cultural center project, President Kennedy ordered it redesigned as a $30 million building and gave his active support to a renewed drive to raise funds. Some $12 million had been raised when he was killed on November 22, 1963.

Following the death of President Kennedy, there was a spontaneous movement throughout the country to make the cultural center, in which he had taken a personal interest, his official memorial in the nation's Capital. Congress approved, changed the center's name to the John F. Kennedy Center for the Performing Arts, and voted $15.5 million for the construction of the building, with an equal sum to come from voluntary contributions. President Lyndon B. Johnson, using the gold spade that had broken ground for the Lincoln and Jefferson me-

morials, broke ground for the John F. Kennedy Center for the Performing Arts on December 2, 1964.

The center building is essentially unchanged from the design approved by President Kennedy in 1962. In addition to excellent facilities for various types of performances, the center has a grand lobby with a beautiful view of the Potomac River that extends the entire two-block length of the building, exhibit areas, restaurants, and other features to add to the pleasure of those who visit it. Honoring as it does a Chief Executive who supported and encouraged the nation's performing artists, the John F. Kennedy Center for the Performing Arts is a fitting memorial to the thirty-fifth President.

Below ground the Washington Monument is supported by a foundation of masonry and poured concrete. This photograph was taken when Army Engineers added concrete to the original masonry foundation during the late 1870's.

Opposite

In this nighttime photograph, the floodlighted Washington Monument and its reflection in the Tidal Basin are framed in the Capital's famous cherry blossoms. The monument is open from 8 A.M. until 11 P.M. during the summer months and from 9 A.M. until 5 P.M. between Labor Day and March 19.

Thousands gather at the foot of the Washington Monument on the evening of Independence Day to watch a brilliant display of fireworks celebrating the signing of the Declaration of Independence in 1776.

Below

Looking southwest across the Potomac River, the nighttime visitor to the Washington Monument sees the lights of the Pentagon and suburban Arlington, Virginia.

Opposite top

The Jefferson Memorial on the south shore of the Tidal Basin completes the plan begun by L'Enfant for the location of the Capital's important buildings and memorials that now include the Capitol, the White House, the Washington Monument, the Lincoln Memorial, and the Jefferson Memorial.

Opposite center

A nineteen-foot statue of the third President by the sculptor Rudulph Evans stands in the center of the Jefferson Memorial. Four panels inscribed with quotations from Jefferson's writings decorate the walls. The memorial is open from 8 A.M. until midnight.

Opposite below

A series of steps leads to the main entrance of the Jefferson Memorial which faces a plaza and the Tidal Basin. The circular, colonnaded structure reflects the third President's taste in architecture. He used a similar circular design for the rotundas of the University of Virginia and for Monticello, his own home.

Our fifteenth President, James Buchanan, is memorialized by a seated bronze statue in garden-like Meridian Hill Park. The park extends from W to Euclid streets on the east side of Sixteenth Street N.W.

The stately Lincoln Memorial in West Potomac Park has been called the most impressive monument in Washington. The thirty-six fluted columns of the exterior colonnade represent the thirty-six states that made up the Union at the time of Lincoln's death. The memorial is especially impressive when lighted at night.

Opposite top
Inside the Lincoln Memorial, a majestic seated figure of Lincoln gazes down on a steady stream of visitors. The statue, carved from twenty-eight blocks of white Georgia marble, was designed by Daniel Chester French.

Opposite center
Voluntary contributions from Negroes financed the Emancipation Monument in Lincoln Park on East Capitol Street between Eleventh and Thirteenth streets N.E. The monument, unveiled in 1876, depicts a standing figure of Lincoln with the Emancipation Proclamation in his right hand. Lincoln's left hand rests on the shoulder of a Negro whose shackles have been broken.

Opposite bottom
In his memorial, Lincoln is represented as a war President deep in contemplation. His Second Inaugural Address has been inscribed on the north wall of the memorial and his Gettysburg Address on the south wall. The memorial is open daily from 8 A.M. until midnight.

Ford's Theatre at 511 Tenth Street N.W. has been restored to look just as it did when John Wilkes Booth shot President Lincoln there on April 14, 1865. The National Park Service administers the theatre and a lower-level Lincoln Museum as a memorial to the martyred President.

Pictures taken by the famous photographer Matthew Brady supplied many of the details needed for an authentic restoration of Ford's Theatre, including the appearance of the box occupied by Lincoln when he was shot (*center right*). The theatre, shown here after the restoration, reopened on February 12, 1968, with a performance of *John Brown's Body*.

President James Garfield is honored by a statue located just west of the Capitol at the intersection of Maryland Avenue and First Street.

Opposite top
A massive memorial to General Ulysses S. Grant, the eighteenth President of the United States, stretches across the Capitol end of the Mall. The 252-foot-long memorial depicts a mounted General Grant looking out over groups of Union artillery and cavalry in action.

Opposite center
Union cavalrymen charge the enemy at one end of the Grant Memorial.

Opposite bottom
These figures of Union soldiers are carved into the central pedestal of the Grant Memorial.

With right hand raised in a characteristic speaking pose, a seventeen-foot-high bronze statue of Theodore Roosevelt looks out over the Roosevelt Memorial.

Opposite top

Roosevelt Island in the Potomac River at the Roosevelt Bridge crossing commemorates Theodore Roosevelt, the nation's twenty-sixth President and a pioneer conservationist. The eighty-eight-acre island is maintained by the National Park Service as a wilderness area. A causeway connects it with the Virginia side of the river.

Opposite bottom

In the impressive Theodore Roosevelt Memorial that occupies the center of Roosevelt Island, four large granite slabs carry quotations from his speeches. The circular memorial also has two curved reflecting pools, beds of boxwood shrubs, stone benches, and a large statue of the twenty-sixth President.

The Theodore Roosevelt Memorial Bridge linking Washington and Virginia passes over the southern tip of Theodore Roosevelt Island. This is the Virginia end of the bridge.

A simple marble block bearing his name and birth and death dates commemorates President Franklin D. Roosevelt on Pennsylvania Avenue near the Archives Building, a site selected by the thirty-second President himself. A more elaborate memorial to President Roosevelt will be erected in West Potomac Park between the Tidal Basin and the river.

The John F. Kennedy Center for the Performing Arts at Rock Creek Parkway and New Hampshire Avenue N.W. is the official memorial in the nation's Capital to the thirty-fifth President of the United States. This view of the east front shows the entrance plaza.

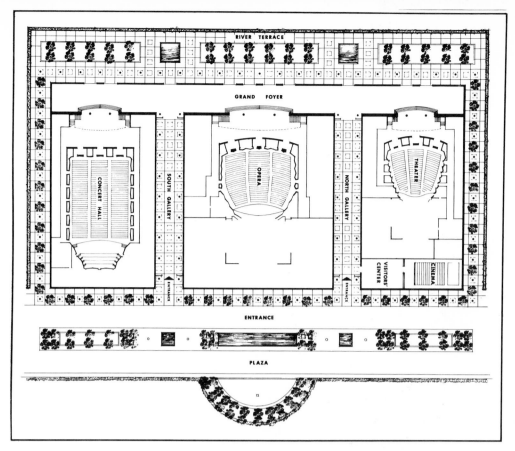

On its main level the Kennedy Center has three large halls
for concerts, opera and ballet, and dramatic productions.

A 110-piece orchestra plus a large chorus can perform on the stage of the Kennedy Center's concert
hall. The hall has seats for 2,700 persons. Its eleven crystal chandeliers were a gift from Norway.

5

CONDUCTING THE EXECUTIVE BUSINESS OF GOVERNMENT

WASHINGTON'S GOVERNMENT BUILDINGS tend toward the monumental, and nowhere is this more in evidence than in the "Federal triangle," an area that extends from a base at Fifteenth Street N.W. to an apex at Sixth, between Pennsylvania and Constitution avenues. Before 1928 a varied assortment of structures lined the triangle's streets. These were torn down in order to carry out the recommendation of the McMillan Commission that the land be cleared and used for government offices.

Between 1928 and 1938, one huge building after another went up in the triangle, most of them six stories high. Although the buildings were designed by different architects, they were planned as a single unit and they all have the same classic and Renaissance architectural details. As a result, the triangle presents an imposing array of colonnades, porticoes, and pediments behind which a host of civil servants conducts the business of government.

Most of the buildings in the triangle house complete government departments, or, in some cases, sections of departments. These departments are part of the executive branch of the United States Government, and their heads, or Secretaries, are members of the President's Cabinet. The Secretaries of Commerce and Labor, the Postmaster General, and the Attorney General all have offices in the triangle, but the Secretary of the Treasury is located just outside of the triangle in the Treasury Building, the oldest of all the departmental buildings.

Although it has the same general architectural style as its neighbors, the National Archives Building near the apex of the triangle has a different function. It houses government records of permanent value. Some of them, like the Declaration of Independence, the Constitution, and the Bill of Rights, are of such value that they are displayed under carefully controlled conditions. Other records are cataloged and placed in the Archives' vast files, where they are available to scholars, writers, and others who wish to consult them.

The Old Post Office Building at Twelfth Street and Pennsylvania Avenue N.W. and the District Building, near the base of the triangle, both predate

Opposite
President Andrew Jackson chose the site for the Treasury Building at Pennsylvania Avenue and Fifteenth Street N.W. Among Washington's government buildings, only the White House and the Capitol are older than the Treasury Building. This is the south portico, one of the main approaches to the building.

the development of the triangle. The Romanesque Old Post Office Building, still used by the Post Office Department along with a larger building nearby, was completed in 1899. The District Building was completed in 1908.

The District Building is Washington's "City Hall." The City Commissioner, usually referred to as the "mayor," his assistant, and the nine-member City Council have offices there along with other members of the city administration. Because of Washington's special status as the seat of the Federal Government, the President appoints the commissioner, his assistant, and the City Council. Residents of Washington have been able to vote for President and Vice President since the 1964 election, but they do not choose their local government officials and they are not represented in Congress. Congress, on the other hand, is empowered by the Constitution "to exercise exclusive Legislation in all Cases whatsoever, over [the] District." This it does through the House and Senate District committees, and by controlling the city's taxing and spending.

Beyond the triangle with its homogeneous structures, government buildings take a variety of forms. In southwest Washington, for example, skilled engravers work on designs for the nation's paper money in the old, romantic-revival Bureau of Engraving Building, where they get more clear, north light than is available in the bureau's newer building on the next block. In Foggy Bottom, so named because it was often covered by "miasmic vapors" arising from nearby swamps (since drained), thousands of government employees work in the modern State Department Building. Meanwhile, the building that State once shared with the War and Navy departments, an elaborately ornate example of nineteenth-century architecture near the White House, continues in service. Now the Executive Office Building, it houses such executive agencies as the National Security Council and the Budget Bureau.

Government buildings are scattered throughout the sixty-nine-square-mile area that makes up the District of Columbia, but the largest one of all—in fact, the largest office building in the world—is located just across the Potomac River in Arlington, Virginia. Built during World War II to house a War Department that had long since outgrown its share of the State, War, and Navy Building, the Pentagon provides office space for upward of 25,000 employees of the Department of Defense, more than half of them civilians.

The Secretary of Defense, an important member of the President's Cabinet, has an office in the Pentagon from which he directs the activities of the Army, Navy, and Air Force in this country and abroad. Assisting him are the civilian Secretaries of the three services and the military Chiefs of Staff, who, with their assistants, are also located in the Pentagon.

In addition to the military and civilian employees of the Defense Department, who are directly engaged in developing and carrying out the country's defense policies, another two or three thousand men and women are needed to keep the Pentagon operating smoothly. In this group are messengers, guards, janitors, and the people who operate such facilities as restaurants, snack bars, banks, stores, gyms, libraries, a printing plant, and other services similar to those that would be provided by a medium-sized city.

In spite of the secret nature of some Pentagon activities, most of the huge building is open to the public, and smiling receptionists are on hand to help visitors find their way through 17½ miles of corridors to the office they seek. There are many visitors each day because the decisions of the Defense Department affect the lives of a great many Americans. Its offices, like those of the other eleven executive departments, are open to any citizen having business with it.

A statue of Alexander Hamilton, the first Secretary of the Treasury, stands at the foot of the Treasury Building's south steps.

Washington's mayor and many of its city officials have offices in the neoclassic District Building at Pennsylvania Avenue and Fourteenth Street N.W.

The Department of Commerce Building, which extends from E Street to Constitution Avenue and from Fourteenth to Fifteenth streets N.W., was the largest office building in Washington when it was completed in 1932.

On the Fourteenth Street side of the Commerce Building a plaza and a large fountain honor Oscar A. Strauss, Secretary of Commerce under President Theodore Roosevelt.

The Bureau of Sport Fisheries and Wildlife maintains a national aquarium in the lower lobby of the Commerce Department Building where many different species of fish are on display in tanks that range from fifty to two thousand gallons in capacity. The aquarium is open daily from 9 A.M. until 5 P.M.

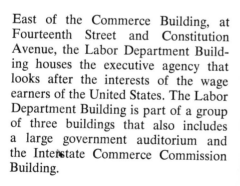

Aquatic reptiles and amphibians are also on display in the national aquarium. Tank decorations simulate the natural environment of each species.

East of the Commerce Building, at Fourteenth Street and Constitution Avenue, the Labor Department Building houses the executive agency that looks after the interests of the wage earners of the United States. The Labor Department Building is part of a group of three buildings that also includes a large government auditorium and the Interstate Commerce Commission Building.

The clock tower on this building is a Washington landmark. It tops the Romanesque Old Post Office Building at Twelfth Street and Pennsylvania Avenue, which once served as Washington's city post office as well as the headquarters of the Post Office Department.

In 1934, the Post Office Department moved its headquarters to this building across Twelfth Street from the old Post Office. The Philatelic Sales Agency and the government stamp collection are both located in the huge hourglass-shaped structure.

The Internal Revenue Service Building at Tenth Street and Constitution Avenue N.W. is typical of the classic, colonnaded architecture of the Federal triangle. The Internal Revenue Service collects all Federal taxes except customs duties.

An inscription on the Department of Justice Building defines the relationship between justice and liberty, both of which are the concern of the department.

JSTICE IS
HE RIGHTS
BY NATURE
LIBERTY IS
IN SECURITY

FOUNDED IN
BESTOWED
UPON MAN.
MAINTAINED
OF JUSTICE.

Since 1934, this large building on Pennsylvania Avenue between Ninth and Tenth streets has been the home of the Department of Justice, the Federal Government's legal arm.

The Justice Department's Federal Bureau of Investigation maintains a number of very popular exhibits in its section of the building. This is part of the F.B.I.'s collection of weapons used by criminals.

Another stop on the F.B.I. tour is the fingerprint laboratory where the world's largest collection of fingerprint cards is available for the identification of criminals. Guided tours are conducted by members of the F.B.I. staff between 9:15 A.M. and 4:15 P.M. on weekdays.

Opposite top
Permanently valuable, noncurrent records of the Federal Government are maintained in the National Archives Building located between Seventh and Ninth streets and Pennsylvania and Constitution avenues N.W. This is the Pennsylvania Avenue side of the building.

Opposite center
An imposing flight of steps leads to the main entrance of the Archives Building on Constitution Avenue. The white marble building with its seventy-two tall Corinthian columns is considered one of the finest examples of classic architecture in Washington.

Opposite below
Carefully sealed in helium-filled cases and protected from harmful light rays, the Declaration of Independence, the Constitution, and the Bill of Rights are on permanent display in the exhibition hall of the National Archives. The students in this picture are some of the many thousands who view the historic documents each year.

In its main exhibition hall and in the corridor running behind it, the National Archives displays important documents selected from its vast collection of historical records. The exhibits are open to the public from 9 A.M. until 10 P.M., Monday through Saturday, and from 1 P.M. until 10 P.M. Sundays.

Standing at the apex of the Federal triangle, the Federal Trade Commission Building is itself an adaptation of a triangular design. It houses the Federal Trade Commission, the government agency charged with preventing unfair practices in business and industry.

At Pennsylvania Avenue and Seventeenth Street N.W., the rococo Executive Office Building reminds passersby of another era when it housed the Departments of State, War, and Navy. The French neo-classic style of the building has been both criticized and praised since its construction during the 1870's. It now provides office space for the Bureau of the Budget, the National Security Council, and other executive agencies.

In this romantic revival building on Fourteenth Street S.W., skilled craftsmen design the nation's currency. The building is not open to the public.

Paper money, stamps, bonds, and other government documents are printed in the factory-like Bureau of Engraving and Printing Building at Fourteenth and C streets S.W. On weekdays, guides show visitors through the building and explain the work of the bureau.

The Department of the Interior Building on C Street between Eighteenth and Nineteenth streets covers more than five acres. The Interior Department Museum on the first floor of the building explains the work of the department which serves as the custodian of the nation's natural resources.

The Department of Transportation Building at 800 Independence Avenue S.W. is an example of the architectural style employed by the designers of Washington's newer government buildings. Its inner walls of glass and metal are movable to provide flexible office areas.

Laws providing a variety of benefits for former members of the Armed Forces are administered from this massive building on Vermont Avenue between H and I streets N.W. The Veterans Administration's regional offices, hospitals, and other centers located throughout the United States make the benefits available to eligible veterans.

Promoting the general welfare of United States citizens in the fields of health, education, and social security is the responsibility of the Department of Health, Education, and Welfare, whose Secretary and staff have offices in this building at 330 Independence Avenue S.W. The Public Health Service, the Office of Education, and the Food and Drug Administration are among the agencies administered by the department.

The National Aeronautics and Space Administration has its headquarters in this building at 400 Maryland Avenue S.W. From here, NASA officials direct the agency's research and development programs in aeronautics and space exploration.

Appropriately enough, the Department of Housing and Urban Development's new building in L'Enfant Plaza has been praised as an outstanding example of urban architecture. The plaza, named for Pierre L'Enfant and located in southwest Washington, is both an office and a shopping center.

This picture of the Department of Agriculture's sprawling buildings on Independence Avenue between Twelfth and Fourteenth streets S.W. was taken from the Washington Monument. The Administration Building is on the left and the South Building is on the right. The Department's agricultural programs include research, education, conservation, marketing, regulatory work, surplus disposal, and rural development.

The Twenty-first Street entrance to the State Department faces one of Washington's many small parks. The main entrance to the building, which houses the executive department responsible for the initiation and implementation of United States foreign policies, is at 2201 C Street N.W.

One hundred and twenty-five guests can be seated in the Benjamin Franklin Dining Room on the eighth floor of the State Department's main building. The eighth floor is used primarily for diplomatic functions.

The State Department Building has two auditoriums. Here, Vice President Hubert Humphrey addresses a group of editors and broadcasters in State's west auditorium.

The Great Seal of the United States, the symbol of our national sovereignty, is on display in an exhibition hall on the first floor of the State Department Building. The seal has been in the custody of the State Department since 1789.

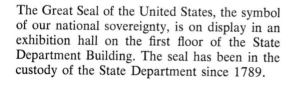

Washington's Fort Lesley J. McNair, located where the Anacostia River flows into the Potomac Channel, is one of the oldest and handsomest Army posts in the country. The fort's entrance is at Fourth and P streets S.W.

The Army War College at Fort McNair provides high-level training for Army officers.

The Naval Observatory at Massachusetts Avenue and Thirty-fourth Street N.W. makes official time measurements for the United States. Regular day tours (Monday through Friday at 2 P.M.) cover the time service and other observatory activities, including its twenty-six-inch telescope. During special night tours at the time of the full moon, visitors can look at the moon through the telescope.

Walter Reed Army Medical Center was named for the famous Army surgeon whose research led to the discovery of the cause of yellow fever. Located at 6823 Sixteenth Street N.W., Walter Reed is a major research center as well as a large hospital. This is the Administration Building, one of the many buildings on its extensive, landscaped grounds.

The largest government building of them all, the Pentagon contains 3,695,130 square feet of office space. The five-sided, five-story building is located in Arlington, Virginia, just across the Fourteenth Street Bridge from Washington. The Secretary of Defense, the Secretaries of the Army, Navy, and Air Force, and the military Chiefs of Staff have offices in the Pentagon along with their sizable staffs. The huge building also has restaurants, snack bars, stores, banks, and many other facilities for the people who work there.

Seven buildings of the Smithsonian Institution
flank the Mall, the parklike expanse of greenery
that extends from the Capitol to the Washington
Monument. The three buildings on the left are,
from the bottom: the Museum of History and
Technology, the Natural History Building, and
the National Gallery of Art. At center right are
(in the same order) the Freer Gallery of Art, the
Air and Space Building, the Smithsonian Building, and the Arts and Industries Building.

6

WASHINGTON'S MUSEUMS

LIKE ITS FEDERAL BUILDINGS, WASHINGTON'S MU-SEUMS belong to the entire country. This is especially true of the many-faceted Smithsonian Institution, which had its origin in a bequest of $550,000 to the United States Government. The donor, James Smithson, was an Englishman who had never visited America. Nevertheless, his will directed that his estate should go to his nephew, and, if the nephew died without leaving an heir, to the United States of America "to found at Washington, under the name of the Smithsonian Institution, an establishment for the increase and diffusion of knowledge among men."

There has been much conjecture as to why Smithson left his money as he did. As a graduate of Oxford and a member of a leading English scientific society, he undoubtedly was interested in science. He may also have been influenced by a desire to compensate for the stigma that his countrymen placed upon his illegitimate birth. Whatever the reason, when Smithson's nephew died childless in 1835, six years after the death of his uncle, the United States fell heir to roughly half a million dollars, a large sum in those days.

After prolonged debate, a Congress unaccustomed to receiving gifts voted to accept the money which, in the form of gold sovereigns, was deposited in the Philadelphia Mint, where it remained until 1846, when Congress passed a bill creating "an institution for the increase and diffusion of knowledge among men." A distinguished scientist, Joseph Henry, was selected to direct the activities of the new Smithsonian Institution, and work began on a "suitable" building.

Congress had decided that the Smithsonian Institution should include a museum, an art gallery, a chemical laboratory, and a library. In 1855 Secretary Henry moved into the Smithsonian Building with a collection of mineralogical specimens, also a bequest from James Smithson. These specimens were the beginning of the present United States National Museum, one of the thirteen bureaus that now make up the Smithsonian Institution. The others are the Astrophysical Observatory, located in Cambridge, Massachusetts; the Tropical Research Institute, in the Canal Zone; and in Washington, the National Zoological Park, the Radiation Biology Laboratory, the International Exchange Service, the Science Information Service, the John F. Kennedy Center for the Performing Arts, the National Air Museum, the Freer Gallery of Art, the National Collection of Fine Arts, the National Portrait Gallery, and the National Gallery of Art.

For most people the Smithsonian consists of the bureaus that have exhibits on display: the National Museum (which includes the Museum of Natural

History and the Museum of History and Technology), the National Air Museum, the Freer Gallery of Art, and the National Gallery of Art, all in buildings bordering the Mall, and the National Collection of Fine Arts and the National Portrait Gallery, both newly located in the old Patent Office Building a few blocks away. While the Smithsonian's education and research activities in Washington, Cambridge, Massachusetts, the Canal Zone, and elsewhere are a very important part of its work, it is the exhibits that attract some fourteen million people a year to the Smithsonian.

The size and scope of the Smithsonian's many exhibits make it the largest museum-gallery complex in the world. It has been estimated that a visitor who spent just one minute on each exhibit would need two and a half years to see everything, and the Smithsonian is still growing. The National Collection of Fine Arts, concentrating on American art, and the National Portrait Gallery, displaying the portraits of men and women who have made significant contributions to the development of the United States, opened in 1968. There will soon be a new National Air and Space Museum on the Mall where many historic airplanes and other items now in storage can be displayed. The National Gallery of Art, originally a gift to the nation by Andrew Mellon, will

be flanked by an addition, given by Mr. Mellon's son and daughter. An entirely new art museum, the Joseph H. Hirshhorn Museum, named for its donor, is planned for a location next to the Arts and Sciences Building, and there are plans for a national sculpture garden, also to be located on the Mall.

In addition to the Smithsonian, Washington has many other galleries and museums which exhibit a wide variety of items. The Corcoran Gallery and its Dupont Center (formerly the Washington Gallery of Modern Art), the Phillips Collection, the Museum of African Art, the Dumbarton Oaks Collection, and the Pan American Union are among those that display works of art. The Truxton-Decatur Naval Museum and the Naval Memorial Museum specialize in relics and memorabilia associated with the United States Navy. In their museum, the Daughters of the American Revolution display period rooms and items of historical interest from early America. The National Historical Wax Museum features important events and famous men from all periods of American history. In its Explorers Hall the National Geographic Society's exhibits are based on its field expeditions and research projects. In these and other museums and galleries there is something to interest everyone who visits the nation's Capital.

When this photograph was taken in 1865, all of the Smithsonian's activities were carried on in the red sandstone Smithsonian Building. The work of architect James Renwick, the turreted structure is considered the finest example of Gothic revival design in the United States.

James Smithson's tomb stands in a small room near the entrance to the Smithsonian Building where it was placed some years after Smithson's death in Italy in 1829.

The Smithsonian's Arts and Industries Building, which has 2½ acres of floor space, cost less than $250,000 when it was finished in 1881. Since then, millions of visitors have viewed its exhibits.

One of the most popular exhibits in the Arts and Industries Building is the original plane that the Wright brothers flew at Kitty Hawk, North Carolina, in 1903. A figure representing Orville Wright occupies the pilot's seat on the lower wing.

The *Spirit of St. Louis,* the monoplane in which Charles Lindbergh made the first nonstop flight from New York to Paris in 1927, now hangs from the rafters in one of the exhibit halls in the Arts and Industries Building.

THE ORIGINAL WRIGHT BROTHERS AEROPLANE, 1903
SEE LABEL BELOW

THE SPIRIT OF ST. LOUIS, 1927

The Hall of Health on the second floor of the Arts and Industries Building features Brünnhilde, the transparent woman whose major organs light up as a recorded lecture explains their functions. There is a performance every fifteen minutes.

Since 1910, the domed Natural History Building has housed the Smithsonian's extensive exhibits and study collections in the fields of anthropology, biology, and geology.

A model of a huge African bush elephant, the largest land mammal of modern times, dominates the rotunda of the Smithsonian's Natural History Building. When alive, the elephant measured more than thirteen feet high at the shoulder and weighed twelve tons. Its hide now covers a papier-mâché form constructed by Smithsonian craftsmen.

Florida was the home of this Timucua Indian warrior on display in the Hall of North American Archeology in the Natural History Building. Details for the construction of the lifelike figure were obtained from a surviving sixteenth-century watercolor and a study of archeological evidence.

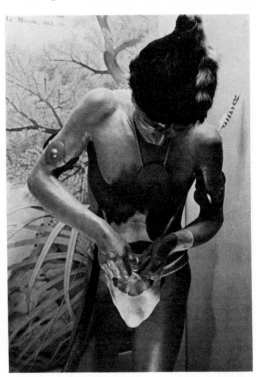

The Smithsonian's special interest in Indians extends beyond the borders of the United States. This hall on the second floor of the Natural History Building features highlights of Latin American archeology.

Wildlife exhibits in the Museum of Natural History are masterpieces of the taxidermist's art. These penguins were collected for the Smithsonian by Admiral Richard E. Byrd's U.S. Antarctic Service.

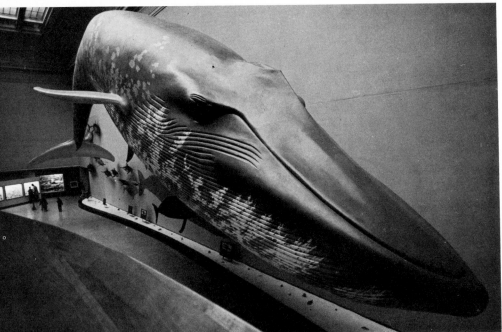

The Museum of Natural History's Hall of Life in the Sea features a life-size model of a ninety-two-foot blue whale caught in the South Atlantic in 1926. The huge whale, the largest mammal that has ever lived, can be seen from below or from a balcony that provides an eye-level view.

Opened in 1964, the Smithsonian's Museum of History and Technology has room for fifty exhibit halls on its three floors. The white marble building was designed to provide maximum wall and window space with a minimum of damaging direct sunlight. The first-floor entrance, shown here, faces Constitution Avenue between Twelfth and Fourteenth streets N.W. The museum has a second-floor entrance facing the Mall.

The famous flag that flew over Fort McHenry during the War of 1812 and inspired Francis Scott Key to write "The Star-Spangled Banner" greets the visitor who enters the Museum of History and Technology from the Mall. The flag, which now measures thirty by twenty-four feet instead of the original thirty by forty-two feet, is one of the Smithsonian's great historical treasures. A painted background fills in the missing sections.

Horatio Greenough's controversial toga-clad statue of George Washington has found a new home on the second floor of the Museum of History and Technology. Installed in the Capitol Rotunda in 1841, it was soon banished to the Capitol's west front, then to the east front and, in 1908, to an unlighted room in the Smithsonian Building. In its new location, the large white marble statue, displayed against a black backdrop, often surprises visitors accustomed to seeing a more conventionally clothed Washington.

No. 1401, the 280-ton, 90-foot-long (with its tender) steam locomotive, had to be moved into place on the first floor of the Museum of History and Technology before the building was completed. At night, the lighted locomotive can be seen through the window. The small steam engine on the left is a wood-burner that dates back to Civil War days.

This 1912 Simplex with bucket seats, right-hand steering, and chain drive is one of several antique cars on display in the Museum of History and Technology's first-floor showroom.

Mannequins wearing gowns that belonged to (from the left) Helen Herron Taft, Edith Kermit Roosevelt, Ida Saxton McKinley, and Frances Folsom Cleveland are displayed in a replica of the White House Blue Room of President McKinley's day. The Blue Room is one of seven rooms in the First Ladies Hall that have been decorated to resemble White House rooms at various periods in United States history.

This 1693 Italian harpsichord is one of the attractions in the Hall of Musical Instruments on the Museum of History and Technology's third floor. On occasion, instruments in the hall are played for museum visitors and music students.

112

Until its new building is completed, the National Air and Space Museum occupies temporary quarters in this gray steel structure near the Arts and Industries Building.

Among the famous aircraft on display in the National Air and Space Building is the *Winnie Mae,* the monoplane in which aviator Wiley Post made two pioneer around-the-world flights in 1931 and 1933.

The space age is represented in the National Air and Space Building by Friendship-7, the space capsule in which Mercury astronaut John Glenn made three orbits around the earth in 1962.

The new National Air and Space Museum Building, planned for a location across the Mall from the National Gallery of Art, will house 313,960 square feet of exhibition area, a 350-seat auditorium, an extensive library, a cafeteria, and other facilities.

Detroit industrialist Charles L. Freer's gift to the nation, the Freer Gallery of Art, occupies a Florentine Renaissance palace on the Mall at Twelfth Street N.W.

The Freer's exhibition galleries surround a graceful open court.

Japanese screens, famous for their design and craftsmanship, line one of the exhibition rooms in the Freer Gallery.

These stone carvings from sixth- and seventh-century China are part of the Freer Gallery's extensive collection of ancient Chinese art.

Covering the three blocks from Fourth to Seventh streets, between Constitution Avenue and Madison Drive, the National Gallery of Art is one of the world's largest art museums. The white marble building was designed by John Russell Pope who also designed the Jefferson Memorial.

The National Gallery's magnificent rotunda with its Mercury fountain and tall columns of green-black marble serves as a fitting introduction to the art treasures in the exhibition rooms.

The National Gallery conducts regularly scheduled tours for its visitors. It also encourages a more leisurely viewing of its masterpieces.

The National Gallery exhibits sculpture as well as painting. The marble urn in the foreground is by the French sculptor Clodion and may have been designed for the palace at Versailles.

Two of the Smithsonian Institution's art galleries, the National Collection of Fine Arts and the National Portrait Gallery, are housed in the old Patent Office Building, one of Washington's most venerable public buildings. The wing occupied by the National Collection of Fine Arts faces G Street N.W. between Seventh and Ninth streets. The National Portrait Gallery wing faces F Street.

The spiral staircase in the National Portrait Gallery is one of the museum's fine architectural details.

Patent models were once displayed in this third-floor hall, now part of the National Portrait Gallery.

The Corcoran Gallery of Art, named for William Wilson Corcoran, the Washington banker who gave his art collection to the city in 1869, occupies a neoclassic building at Seventeenth Street and New York Avenue N.W. The Corcoran's collections emphasize American art but include Dutch, Flemish, English, and French works as well. The gallery is open from 10 A.M. until 4:30 P.M. Tuesday through Friday, 9 A.M. until 4:30 P.M. Saturday, and 2 P.M. until 5 P.M. Sundays and holidays.

This is one of the Corcoran's spacious, well-lighted galleries devoted to American art.

Rembrandt Peale's large canvas "Washington Before Yorktown" overlooks the Corcoran Gallery's Clark staircase, named for William Andrews Clark whose large art collection is housed in one wing of the gallery. The Clark Collection includes French, Dutch, and Flemish paintings, French tapestries, Persian and other rugs, European laces, antique figurines, and a reconstructed Paris salon from the time of Louis XVI.

In the converted mansion of the Phillips family at 1600 Twenty-first Street N.W. and a contemporary annex at 1612 Twenty-first Street, the Phillips Collection displays modern art and works that illustrate its sources.

The Phillips Collection hangs its paintings in softly lighted rooms that invite leisurely inspection. These paintings are by Georges Braque.

Important events in United States naval history are featured at the Truxtun-Decatur Naval Museum at 1610 H Street N.W. The museum, a project of the Naval Historical Foundation, is open from 10:30 A.M. until 4 P.M., Tuesday through Sunday.

Authentic ship models play important part in the Na Museum's displays. This mo of the U.S.S. *Olympia*, A miral Dewey's flagship at M nila Bay, was part of an exhi based on the Spanish-Am ican War.

The Truxtun-Decatur Naval Museum occupies what was once the carriage house of historic Decatur House. The museum carries the names of two early American naval heroes, Commodore Thomas Truxtun and Commodore Stephen Decatur. The latter also gave his name to Decatur House.

Dramatic scenes from American history are featured in the exhibit halls of the National Historical Wax Museum at Fifth and K streets N.W. Here, four World War II Army chaplains give up their life belts and remain behind while others escape from the torpedoed troopship *Dorchester*.

A popular Wax Museum tableau shows Meriwether Lewis and William Clark of the Lewis and Clark Expedition to the Pacific Northwest, and some of the Indians who helped them.

Exhibits in the Bible History Wax Museum, adjacent to the National Historical Wax Museum, are based on events described in the Old and New Testaments. This scene depicts the birth of Christ in Bethlehem.

Textiles dating from the second millennium B.C. are on display in the Textile Museum at 2320 S Street N.W. In addition to textiles from all over the world, the museum's collections include a large number of fine oriental rugs.

One of Washington's unique museums is a reproduction of Christopher Columbus' flagship, the *Santa Maria,* docked at Pier 3 on the Maine Avenue waterfront. Among the attractions of the authentically-equipped ship-museum are life-size figures dressed as members of the *Santa Maria*'s crew and twelve large dioramas illustrating the life of Columbus.

Washington's West Potomac Park, shown here in the spring with the famous Japanese cherry trees in bloom, has some of the city's most beautiful scenery and miles of walks from which to enjoy it. Part of the Tidal Basin can be seen on the right.

7

PARKS, CIRCLES, AND SQUARES

PARKS HAVE BEEN AN IMPORTANT PART OF THE NATION'S CAPITAL ever since Major L'Enfant drew the original plans for the city. With George Washington's approval, L'Enfant reserved land surrounding the Capitol and the President's House for parks and proposed connecting them with a long, open parkway which later became the Mall. In various sections of the future city scenic areas were set aside for large parks. Small parks in the form of circles and squares were planned for the intersections of avenues and streets. In general, L'Enfant's proposals have been carried out, giving Washington an exceptionally fine parks system.

Because the Capital's 7,697 acres of park lands are Federal property, they are supervised and maintained by the Federal Government through the Interior Department's National Park Service. Before the Park Service took over in 1933, the parks were administered by a number of Federal agencies, including, between 1867 and 1925, the War Department.

Washington's oldest park, the Mall, began as L'Enfant's "grand avenue," of which he wrote: "This avenue leads to the Monument and connects the Congress Garden with the President's Park." The monument that L'Enfant mentioned was to have been placed some three hundred feet from the site of the Washington Monument, but soil conditions made building there impossible. L'Enfant envisioned

the Mall as a broad street bordered with gardens and spacious houses "such as may accommodate foreign ministers, etc.," but the Mall developed into a clutter of trees, gardens, grass plots, and a variety of buildings including the turreted, red sandstone Smithsonian Building.

During the 1850's the first tentative steps were taken toward the development of the Mall as an informal, landscaped park. A big improvement occurred in 1901 when the McMillan Commission persuaded the two railways whose tracks crossed the Mall to remove them and their passenger stations to a new terminal northeast of the Capitol, the present Union Station. The McMillan Commission also recommended that a proposed memorial to Abraham Lincoln be erected one mile west of the Washington Monument on land dredged from the Potomac. This had the effect of extending the Mall by one mile, so that today it stretches from the Capitol to the Potomac River and covers 256 acres.

Officially, the Lincoln Memorial and its grounds are part of West Potomac Park, 394 acres of drained swampland that make up one of Washington's most popular parks. Here are the reflecting pool, a shallow, rectangular basin designed to enhance the setting of the Lincoln Memorial; the Tidal Basin, a quiet landlocked pool of water fed by the Potomac tides; and the famous Japanese cherry trees.

The first of Washington's cherry trees arrived from Japan in 1912, the gift of the city of Tokyo. Mrs. Howard Taft, the wife of the President, personally planted one of the trees on the edge of the Tidal Basin and the wife of the Japanese Ambassador planted another. The trees, with their beautiful pink and white blossoms, quickly became famous, drawing thousands of springtime visitors to Washington. During the 1930's the city began to hold a cherry blossom festival during the week that, hopefully, the cherry trees were in full bloom. Although it is difficult to predict the time of blooming, the cherry blossom festival has become a popular annual event with a pageant, a parade, and cherry blossom princesses selected from each state. One of them, chosen by lot, reigns over the festival as queen.

Since the original planting, additional cherry trees have been added from time to time, and trees have also been planted in East Potomac Park, a scenic, 327-acre peninsula that adjoins West Potomac Park.

Now much used by golfers, tennis players, and picnickers, East Potomac Park will soon have another attraction. The new National Fisheries Center and Aquarium, authorized by Congress in 1962, will be built there. The aquarium will reproduce an acre of the Florida Everglades in a semicircular glass enclosure as one of its displays of living aquatic ecologies, demonstrating the interplay of life in and around water.

Across the city from the Potomac parks, the National Arboretum offers several miles of trails that wind through some of Washington's most beautiful floral displays. The Department of Agriculture administers the Arboretum as a plant research center and as an outdoor museum where many different kinds of trees, shrubs, and other plants can be studied. Although it is not a part of Washington's parks system, the Arboretum is open to the public daily, with longer hours during special periods, such as when its famous azaleas are in bloom.

Another of Washington's garden areas, the Kenilworth Aquatic Gardens, on the Anacostia River in northeast Washington, features fourteen acres of ponds in which a profusion of colorful water lilies and lotuses grow. Some of the lotuses were raised from Manchurian seeds estimated to be one thousand years old. The gardens also contain other examples of pond, marsh, and river plants and many

birds and small animals.

Kenilworth, which began as the hobby of a government clerk and developed into one of the largest commercial enterprises of its kind, was acquired by the National Park Service in 1938. The gardens are open daily, and on summer weekends a Park Service naturalist is on hand to conduct bird and flower walks.

Washington's largest park, the eighteen-hundred-acre Rock Creek Park, borders winding Rock Creek in the northwest part of the city. Congress made the area a park in 1890, declaring it "A pleasure ground for the people of the United States." Today the wooded park contains a variety of small animals, many birds, and, among other attractions, historic Pierce Mill, the cabin in which poet Joaquin Miller lived, and the National Park Service's Rock Creek Nature Center, which features work-it-yourself exhibits, illustrated talks, self-guiding nature trails, and a planetarium, all designed to promote an understanding of the world of nature.

The National Zoological Park, a bureau of the Smithsonian Institution, borders Rock Creek Park on the south. Its collection, which now numbers over three thousand living mammals, birds, and reptiles, began with a few animals which the Smithsonian kept penned on the Mall to serve as models for its taxidermists. As their number increased, so did the interest of the public in the living animals, and the need arose for larger quarters. Secretary Samuel P. Langley of the Smithsonian asked Congress to provide a zoological park, which Congress did in 1889. When the zoo opened in 1890, a herd of American bison, a species then threatened with extinction, joined the animals moved from the Mall. Over the years other animals have come to the National Zoological Park as the result of gifts, purchases, exchanges with other zoos, field expeditions, and births at the zoo. Smithsonian scientists conduct research at the zoo, and millions of people from all over the country visit its exhibits every year, making it truly a national zoo.

These are just a few of the many parks, large and small, that provide a setting of beauty for Washington's buildings and monuments. As national parks, their floral displays and landscaped greenery are designed not only to enhance buildings and monuments, but to give pleasure to the nation's citizens as well.

McPherson Square on Fifteenth Street, between I and K streets N.W., is one of the many small parks scattered throughout Washington. It was named for Civil War General James B. McPherson whose statue can be seen in the background.

Boating on the Tidal Basin is a popular Washington pastime. The Tidal Basin was created at the same time that marshland along the Potomac River was drained to make East and West Potomac parks.

A bronze statue of Alexander R. Shepherd stands on a triangular green plot near the District Building. As a member of the Board of Public Works during the 1870's, Shepherd was responsible for many badly needed civic improvements.

Golfers at the East Potomac Park course play within sight of the Capitol. The park also has facilities for tennis, swimming, and picnicking.

From East Potomac Park's willow-bordered walks, strollers can look across the Potomac Channel to Fort Lesley J. McNair.

The National Park Service's Hains Point Visitor Information Center in East Potomac Park provides folders, exhibits, and movies about Washington, as well as general information on the attractions of the nation's Capital.

Boy Scouts throughout the nation contributed money to pay for their national monument on the Fifteenth Street side of the Ellipse. The bronze monument with its uniformed scout and figures representing American manhood and womanhood stands on a marble pedestal at one end of a large oval pool.

John Witherspoon, a signer of the Declaration of Independence, is honored by a bronze statue at Connecticut Avenue and N Street N.W.

Dupont Circle, at the intersection of Connecticut, Massachusetts, and New Hampshire avenues, is perhaps the best known of Washington's many traffic circles. Once a fashionable residential area of great mansions, Dupont Circle has become a gathering place for young people. The circle and its central fountain honor Rear Admiral Samuel F. Du Pont, a Civil War naval hero.

A bronze figure of Daniel Webster, the American statesman and orator, looks out over Scott Circle from the west.

General Winfield Scott's statue in Scott Circle, at the intersection of Massachusetts and Rhode Island avenues and Sixteen and N streets N.W., was cast from cannon captured during the Mexican War, the conflict that made the general famous.

Although no picnicking is allowed in the National Arboretum, areas of unusual beauty are well supplied with benches.

Signs direct National Arboretum visitors over nine miles of paved roads leading to the principal plant groups. The main entrance to the 415-acre Arboretum is just east of the point where Maryland Avenue N.E. terminates at M Street.

The Arboretum's dogwoods are a popular attraction during late April and early May when they are in flower.

At Connecticut Avenue and Eighteenth Street
N.W., a seated statue of the poet Henry W. Long-
fellow looks out over a shady little park.

Night-blooming tropical water lilies are among the many attractions at the Kenilworth Aquatic Gardens in northeast Washington. The lilies open in late July or
August.

The Arboretum's azalea plantings are among the most extensive in the nation. They bloom during April and May.

POINT FOR THE
MEASUREMENT
OF · DISTANCES
FROM · WASHING
TON · ON · HIGH
WAYS · OF · THE
UNITED · STATES

Although it is officially part of the White House grounds, the Ellipse, a grassy area south of the White House, is open to the public for park use. The annual Pageant of Peace, with the President lighting the national Christmas tree, is held on the Ellipse. Two views.

As founder and chairman of the Committee for a More Beautiful Washington, Mrs. Lyndon B. Johnson took an active part in improving the appearance of the nation's Capital. She is shown here with one of the magnolia trees planted along Pennsylvania Avenue as a result of the efforts of the committee.

Count Casimir Pulaski, Polish hero of the American Revolution, has been memorialized with an equestrian statue in Pulaski Park at Thirteenth Street and Pennsylvania Avenue N.W.

This photograph shows some of the detail of Polish sculptor Casimir Chodzinski's Pulaski statue.

In the lower or Italian section of Meridian Hill Park, a water cascade descends over thirteen steps to a small pool. Meridian Hill, which has a French as well as an Italian section, is one of Washington's most charming parks.

Before 1912, Anacostia Park was an unhealthy stretch of marshland bordering the Anacostia River. Reclamation changed the former Anacostia Flats into a scenic urban park.

The United States Capitol supplies the backdrop for the Peace Monument in the traffic circle at Pennsylvania Avenue and First Street N.W. The monument, erected in honor of members of the United States Navy who fell in the Civil War, is surmounted by a symbolic figure representing America who weeps on the shoulder of "History" for her heroic dead.

Just north of the Ellipse, a bronze figure of "Winged Victory" tops an eighty-foot memorial column whose base carries the names of members of the Army's First Infantry Division who died in World War I and World War II.

Farragut Square, bounded by Seventeenth, I, and K streets N.W., is a small green park surrounded by office buildings. The statue of Civil War hero Admiral David G. Farragut in the background was cast from metal from his flagship, the *Hartford*. Farragut, the United States Navy's first admiral, is remembered for his famous words at Mobile Bay: "Damn the torpedoes! Full speed ahead!"

Benjamin Franklin gazes down upon Washington traffic from a small plaza at the intersection of Pennsylvania Avenue with Tenth and D streets N.W.

The state of Pennsylvania commissioned this statue of Civil War General George Meade at the Capitol end of the Mall. Standing on a round pedestal, the general is thrusting aside a symbolic figure of War in favor of a figure representing Peace.

One of Rock Creek Park's many attractions is Pierce Mill, which dates back to about 1820. Now restored, it is open to the public as a fine example of the water-powered gristmills that once ground America's grain.

During the summer months, Washingtonians go to Rock Creek Park's Carter Barron Amphitheatre for a variety of entertainment that includes musicals, operettas, symphony concerts, folk music, and ballets. A concessionaire operates the open-air theatre for the National Park Service.

Opposite
Rock Creek, shown here in the wintertime, rises in Maryland and flows south through a wooded gorge to join the Potomac River a few blocks west of the White House. Rock Creek gives its name to Rock Creek Park, Washington's largest park.

Smokey the Bear is probably the most famous resident of the National Zoological Park. Rescued from an Arizona forest fire as a cub, Smokey has been featured on television and radio programs and on posters as a symbol of forest fire prevention and wildlife conservation. Smokey's ranger hat, belt, trousers, and shovel are displayed near his cage.

Another famous resident of the National Zoological Park is Mohini Rewa, a rare white tiger from India.

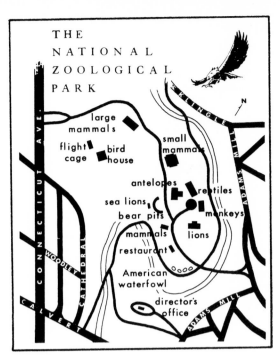

Ham, the chimpanzee who made a sixteen-minute sub-orbital flight for Project Mercury in 1961, has retired to the National Zoological Park after a successful career as a space pioneer.

Adjoining Rock Creek Park on the south, the National Zoological Park, Washington's zoo, covers 175 wooded acres.

Following the course of Rock Creek for part of the way, the Rock Creek and Potomac Parkway extends from the west side of the Lincoln Memorial to the National Zoological Park. It has facilities for riding, fishing, and picnicking.

Washington's "Church of the Presidents" is venerable St. John's Episcopal Church in Lafayette Square. Since President James Madison rented Pew 54 in the then new church in 1817, most Chief Executives have attended at least some services there. Pew 54 is still reserved for Presidential use.

8
SOME WASHINGTON CHURCHES AND COLLEGES

ALTHOUGH WASHINGTON'S CHIEF BUSINESS IS GOVERNMENT, it is also a religious center of note. The city has numerous churches representing many different denominations. Several national churches have been built in Washington, and religious organizations have located their headquarters here. A number of Washington churches are almost as well known in other parts of the country as they are in the Capital, some because they are important for historical reasons and others because they are national churches.

Much photographed St. John's Episcopal Church in Lafayette Square has been the "church of the Presidents" since James Madison rented a pew there in 1817. The church is also famous for its Federal-style architecture, designed by Benjamin Latrobe, who contributed to both the White House and the Capitol. The versatile Latrobe was St. John's first organist.

Benjamin Latrobe also designed another of Washington's historic churches, Christ Church at 620 G Street S.E. Presidents Madison, Jefferson, and John Quincy Adams attended its services.

Washington Cathedral, officially the Cathedral Church of St. Peter and St. Paul, is one of Washington's national churches. As such, it is the seat of the bishop of the Protestant Episcopal Church, but many of its services are interdenominational. The cathedral, constructed in the Gothic style of the great European religious structures of the Middle Ages, is one of the world's largest churches. It contains several chapels, including three crypt chapels symbolizing the birth, death, and resurrection of Christ. The chapels and the main body of the church are richly decorated in the Gothic tradition, and a number of distinguished Americans, including President Woodrow Wilson, have been buried in the cathedral.

As its name suggests, the National Shrine of the Immaculate Conception is another national church, belonging to Catholics all over the United States, thousands of whom come to Washington each year to worship in the shrine and to enjoy its elaborate exterior and interior ornamentation. Like the Washington Cathedral, the Shrine of the Immaculate Conception is still unfinished, although construction has been under way for many years.

Designed in the shape of a Latin cross, the shrine combines details of Byzantine and Romanesque architecture. A striking Byzantine dome rises to 237 feet and a slender bell tower to 329 feet. The interior of the church contains many works of art including, in the arched apse behind the main altar, one of the world's largest mosaics of Christ. Beneath the main church is the smaller crypt church, the first part of the shrine to be completed. Ceremonies there are conducted from a beautiful altar of semitransparent golden onyx.

The National Shrine is open to the public daily, and there are frequent guided tours of its numerous points of interest.

People from many foreign countries attend Washington's churches and, for them, services are conducted in about two dozen different languages in churches, mosques, synagogues, and temples scattered throughout the city.

One of the most colorful of these is the mosque at the Islamic Center in northwest Washington. In addition to the mosque, which is angled to face the Holy Kaaba at Mecca in Saudi Arabia, the center contains the Islamic Institute, which uses its library, classrooms, and auditorium to promote understanding of the Moslem world. All of the Moslem countries with diplomatic missions in Washington helped pay for the Islamic Center, and the many works of art that decorate the mosque were donated by them.

Washington has some unique advantages as an educational center for both church-affiliated and independent colleges and universities. The Federal Government's libraries and archives provide a vast reservoir of research material and its experts in many fields are available for lectures and consultation. The presence in Washington of many private research organizations and foundations adds to the city's advantages as an educational center.

The George Washington University, with an enrollment exceeding twelve thousand, is the Capital's largest institution of higher education. It began as Baptist-affiliated Columbian College, to which Congress granted a charter in 1821 for the "sole and exclusive purpose of educating youth in the English, learned and foreign languages, the liberal arts, sciences, and literature." President Monroe and his Cabinet attended the first commencement.

The college moved several times, dropped its Baptist affiliation, and changed its name to The George Washington University before settling in its present downtown Washington campus bounded by G and E and Twenty-first and Twenty-second streets N.W.

More than ten thousand students attend The

American University, which has a large campus in northwest Washington and a downtown graduate center. The American University is a nonsectarian school with a Methodist affiliation.

The Catholic University of America in northeast Washington is administered by the Roman Catholic bishops of the United States as the national Catholic university. Its students include many members of religious orders whose houses are located on or near the university's large campus.

Georgetown University, founded in 1789, is the oldest Catholic university in the United States and the oldest of Washington's colleges and universities. It differs from Catholic University in that it is administered by the Jesuit religious order and financed by gifts and student tuition rather than church funds. The university's School of Foreign Service is one of the best in the country.

Washington's Howard University was founded in 1867 as a seminary for training Negro men for the ministry. It bears the name of General Oliver Otis Howard, who helped obtain Federal funds to establish the school. Today Howard's ten schools and colleges are supported by congressional appropriations and private funds. Howard admits students of every race, creed, color, and national origin, but it accepts a special responsibility for the training of Negro students, and it has graduated large numbers of Negro doctors, dentists, pharmacists, lawyers, engineers, teachers, and social workers.

Another Washington school partly supported by Federal funds is Gallaudet College, which provides a liberal education in the arts and sciences for deaf persons. Since Gallaudet is the world's only school of higher education for the deaf, some of its students come from foreign countries.

Washington's newest college, the Federal City College, opened in 1968. It is the Capital's first public liberal arts college and offers both a two-year junior college and a four-year senior college program. The new school admits anyone with a high-school diploma, but high nonresident tuition limits the number of its out-of-city students.

In addition to its five large universities and the new Federal City College, Washington has a number of smaller liberal arts colleges, as well as a great many schools that offer special training of various kinds.

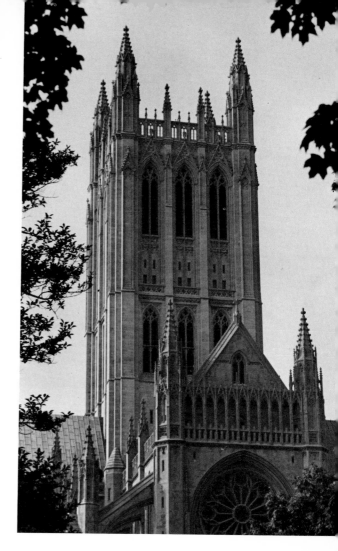

Washington Cathedral, officially the Cathedral Church of St. Peter and St. Paul, has been under construction since 1907 and is still unfinished. The cathedral is located at Massachusetts and Wisconsin avenues N.W. on Mount St. Alban, one of the highest elevations in the District of Columbia.

Top right
Washington Cathedral's three-hundred-foot Gloria in Excelsis Tower has two sets of bells, a fifty-three-bell carillon and a ten-bell ring. The carillon is played from a manual and pedal keyboard, but the bells are rung individually by hand.

Like all Gothic structures, Washington Cathedral has an abundance of decorations and embellishments, the work of skilled sculptors, stonecutters, and woodcarvers.

A golden equestrian statue of George Washington stands on a landscaped plaza on the cathedral grounds. Also on the fifty-seven acres of grounds that surround the cathedral are a parish church, a College of Preachers (for postgraduate training of clergy), the College of Church Musicians (interdenominational advanced training for organists and choirmasters), Beauvoir, the Cathedral elementary school, St. Alban's School for Boys, and the National Cathedral School for Girls.

Right
The high dome of St. Matthew's, topped by a slender lantern and a Latin cross, is a Washington landmark.

St. Matthew's Cathedral is familiar to many Americans as the scene of funeral services for President John F. Kennedy on November 25, 1963. The cathedral is located at 1725 Rhode Island Avenue N.W., a few blocks from the White House.

Christ Church at 620 G Street S.E. dates back to 1807 which makes it one of Washington's oldest churches. Architect Benjamin Latrobe designed the building, although it has been considerably altered over the years. The Congressional Cemetery occupies part of the Christ Church burial ground.

The Islamic Center with its white mosque and 160-foot-high minaret brings a touch of the Near East to Washington. Located at 2551 Massachusetts Avenue N.W., the mosque is the house of worship for approximately three thousand Moslems who live in the Washington area. The mosque is open to visitors who, like the worshipers, must remove their shoes before entering.

The National City Christian Church on Thomas Circle was designed by John Russell Pope, the architect of the Archives Building. The church is Washington headquarters for the Disciples of Christ.

The white limestone National Memorial Baptist Church at Sixteenth Street and Columbia Road N.W. was erected in the early 1920's as a national memorial to religious liberty.

Built in thanksgiving for the end of the Civil War, the red sandstone Luther Place Memorial Church faces the National City Church across Thomas Square. Civil War General George H. Thomas' statue is on the right. The smaller statue in front of the church honors Martin Luther.

Dr. William Thornton, the architect of the Capitol, also drew the plans for St. John's Church at O and Potomac streets in Georgetown. The original design of the church has been greatly modified since the building was dedicated in 1809, but it remains one of Washington's historic churches.

Financed by contributions from Catholics all over the United States, the National Shrine of the Immaculate Conception is a national, rather than a parish, church and the largest Catholic church in the country. It is located on the campus of Catholic University in northeast Washington.

These carvings at the entrance to the National Shrine of the Immaculate Conception are an example of its lavishly decorated exterior. The church is built entirely of stone and masonry.

The central aisle of the National Shrine of the Immaculate Conception is three hundred feet long. Three thousand people can be seated in the shrine and a total of six thousand accommodated. A special public-address system carries the services to all parts of the vast church.

The Franciscan Monastery Memorial Church of the Holy Land contains replicas of sacred shrines of the Holy Land and underground catacombs modeled after those in Rome. The monastery, located at Fourteenth and Quincy streets N.E., includes the church, its adjoining cloister, and forty-four acres of grounds.

A series of arcades, called the Rosary Portico, surround the Memorial Church of the Holy Land. The arcades contain chapels and memorial panels.

St. Christopher bearing the infant Christ on his shoulders is one of the many statues that decorate the monastery grounds.

In a setting of fruit and shade trees, flowering shrubs, vineyards, and, in early summer, a beautiful rose garden, the Franciscans have built a number of outdoor shrines dedicated to persons and events connected with the life of Christ.

The Franciscan Monastery's Grotto of Gethsemane reproduces the original in Jerusalem where Christ retired with his disciples on the eve of the Crucifixion. The monastery is open to the public daily and guides are available.

The George Washington University campus centers on the Yard, a landscaped area surrounded by university buildings. Building C is on the left and Corcoran Hall on the right. The university is located at Twentieth and G streets N.W.

The American University seventy-five-acre campus at Massachusetts and Nebraska avenues N.W. occupies the former site of Fort Gaines, a Civil War fort. The circular structure in the background is the Spiritual Life Center, one of the university's many new buildings.

Hurst Hall, named for Methodist Episcopal Bishop John Fletcher Hurst who was instrumental in raising funds to purchase land for American's uptown campus, is the university's oldest building. The imposing white marble structure was completed in 1898, but the university did not move into it until 1925.

American University's art students attend classes in the modern Watkins Art Building.

Established in 1889 with the approval of Pope Leo XIII, The Catholic University of America has important science and art departments, as well as religious schools on its large campus in northeast Washington. The National Shrine of the Immaculate Conception (*left*) serves as the university church.

Catholic University's Romanesque John K. Mullen Memorial Library contains more than 634,000 volumes, including important collections of Biblical works.

McMahon Hall is one of Catholic University's oldest buildings. Located in the center of the campus, it houses classrooms, laboratories, offices, an auditorium, and the campus store.

Georgetown University's well-known medical and dental schools share a colonial-style building in the northern part of the campus.

Georgetown University overlooks the Potomac River from the crest of a bluff. The main entrance to the eighty-acre campus is at Thirty-seventh and O streets, in the western part of Georgetown.

Visible from many parts of the city, the Healy Building's Victorian Gothic tower is one of Washington's landmarks.

The Healy Building (*left*) is Georgetown University's administrative headquarters. The Copley Building is on the right.

Howard University, with more than eight thousand students, is one of Washington's largest universities. It enrolls a greater percentage of foreign students than any other American university. This is the main entrance to the campus. The building in the right background is the library.

The Georgian architecture of Howard University's Main Hall (*right*) is typical of the older buildings on its campus at 2400 Sixth Street N.W. The university celebrated its one-hundredth anniversary in 1967.

The Chemistry Building houses some of the two hundred modern laboratories that are available to Howard students.

The College of Fine Arts is one of the ten schools and colleges that make up Howard University. This is the Fine Arts Building.

Objects of African tribal art and works of Negro artists are displayed in the Howard University Gallery of Art, a part of the university's College of Fine Arts. The gallery's permanent exhibits include the African art collection of Dr. Alain LeRoy Locke who was on the Howard faculty from 1912 until 1953.

Italian Renaissance paintings, the gift of Samuel H. Kress, are on display at the Howard University Gallery. Kress, a noted art collector, also gave paintings to the National Gallery of Art.

Gallaudet College at Seventh Street and Florida Avenue N.E. provides higher education for deaf persons who need special facilities to compensate for their loss of hearing. The building in the background is College Hall, the main building on the campus.

Frederick Law Olmsted, the famous landscape architect, laid out the Gallaudet College grounds in 1886.

A statue representing Dr. Thomas Hopkins Gallaudet teaching his first pupil stands in front of College Hall. Gallaudet (1787–1851) was a pioneer teacher of the deaf.

The Old Stone House (*center*) at 3051 M Street in Georgetown is one of the oldest buildings in the nation's Capital. A fine example of pre-Revolutionary architecture, the 1765 house is now administered by the National Park Service and is open to the public Wednesday through Saturday, from 1 to 5 P.M.

From M Street the Old Stone House appears to be very small, but a side view gives a better indication of its size. Some of the Old Stone House's eight rooms have been restored and furnished in the style of the late eighteenth century.

9

A CITY OF
VARIED ARCHITECTURE

Nongovernmental Washington offers a number of attractions that are at once complimentary to and different from the Washington of the Capitol, the White House, and the Federal triangle. One of them is Georgetown, a settled community long before the Revolutionary War, where a colonial atmosphere still lingers.

Georgetown, which grew up on the site of an old Indian village, prospered from the beginning because of its location at the head of Potomac navigation. For many years, Georgetown ships carried tobacco to ports in Europe and the West Indies and returned with goods for Maryland and Virginia planters. A successful gun factory and a large flour mill added to its prosperity.

Georgetown's wealthy citizens built fine houses, many of them on the wooded hills overlooking the Potomac River. When the first government officials moved to the rough, new Federal city in 1800, they were delighted to rent or buy a house in Georgetown, from which they traveled to the Capital in a stagecoach that made one round trip a day. There are a number of houses and other buildings still standing in Georgetown that date from the years around the turn of the century, but the Old Stone House on M Street is one of the few remaining structures that predate the Revolutionary War.

Although most of Georgetown's historic houses are private residences, to be visited only during special house or garden tours, a few are open to the public on a regular basis. The Old Stone House, administered by the National Park Service, is one of these, as is Dumbarton House, at 2715 Q Street, which the Society of Colonial Dames has restored, and Dumbarton Oaks at 3101 R Street. The latter was given to Harvard University by its last private owners. The university now maintains the elegant mansion as a center for the study of the early Christian and Byzantine periods and as a museum.

Georgetown's early prosperity did not outlast the first half of the nineteenth century. The advent of the steamship ended its ocean trade, and the new railroads helped ruin the Chesapeake and Ohio Canal in which Georgetown citizens had invested heavily. The town deteriorated into an increasingly shabby suburb of Washington, and in 1871 it became an official part of the Capital city. Georgetown's decline ended in the 1920's and 1930's, when it was rediscovered by writers, artists, and government employees, who bought its old houses and restored them. Land values soared as Georgetown once more became a fashionable place to live.

Because Georgetowners keep a watchful eye on what happens in their community, they have generally succeeded in preserving the town's distinctive character, which adds a unique quality to the Capital scene.

Another source of the variety that is to be found in Washington is the presence in the city of the national headquarters of many organizations. Among them is the American Institute of Architects, which has its headquarters in historic Octagon House, a Georgian town house dating from 1800 that had become a run-down tenement when the institute took it over in 1900. The architects have restored the house and equipped it with furnishings from the early 1800's, the period when Octagon House was the center of Washington's social activity and, after the White House burned in 1814, the temporary home of President Madison and his wife, Dolley.

The world's largest scientific and educational organization, the National Geographic Society, has its headquarters in a modern, white marble building at Seventeenth and M streets, one of several new hotel and office buildings that have gone up in Washington's midtown area. Although most of the National Geographic Building is devoted to office space, an Explorers Hall on the first floor presents exhibits based on the society's explorations and scientific work. The hall is open to the public daily.

More than 184,000 women, descendants of Revolutionary War patriots, have their national headquarters on Seventeenth Street west of the White House, where three buildings belonging to the Daughters of the American Revolution occupy an entire city block. Every spring during the week that includes April 19, the anniversary of the Battle of Lexington, the organization holds its convention in its handsome Constitution Hall, a well-equipped auditorium which, during the rest of the year, is used for concerts by the National Symphony Orchestra and other events. The D.A.R.'s Memorial Continental Hall contains a 51,000-volume genealogical library that can be consulted by the general public and authentically decorated period rooms. In the organization's third building is a museum specializing in early Americana.

The D.A.R.'s headquarters are flanked on the north by the headquarters of the American Red Cross and on the south by the Pan American Union. The latter houses the headquarters of the Organization of American States in a beautiful building that was designed and decorated to represent all the countries of the Americas.

More than a hundred foreign governments have diplomatic missions in Washington, and their presence adds an exotic touch to the Capital. The various embassies and legations are clustered in northwest Washington with both Massachusetts Avenue and Sixteenth Street qualifying as "embassy rows," but diplomatic missions are located on other streets as well.

Some embassies occupy mansions that once belonged to wealthy Washingtonians. The former home of successful gold miner Thomas F. Walsh, whose daughter was the last private owner of the Smithsonian Institution's famous Hope diamond, became the Indonesian Embassy. The Soviet Embassy belonged to the widow of railroad-car tycoon George Pullman, and the Embassy of Brazil occupies the former home of newspaper magnate Robert S. McCormick. The taking over of these and other distinguished Washington mansions by foreign diplomatic missions has probably saved them from destruction, since they had become too expensive for private ownership.

Many countries have built their own embassies and chanceries in Washington and, as a result, a variety of foreign architectural styles can be seen in the city. The British Embassy on Massachusetts Avenue resembles an English country house. The Italian Embassy on Fuller Street was designed in the Italian Renaissance style. When the Japanese built their Massachusetts Avenue Embassy, they chose colonial architecture, but they added an authentic Japanese teahouse to the garden. Oil-rich Kuwait's Embassy on Tilden Street is in the architectural style of the Middle East. Denmark and the Federal Republic of Germany have erected modern structures in Washington, the Danes a combination ambassador's residence and chancery on Whitehaven Street, and the Germans a chancery on Reservoir Road. Both have been praised as among the best of Washington's contemporary buildings.

While there is indeed much that is to be commended in the nation's Capital, there are also many things that need to be improved. The slums that once covered the southwest section of the city have been replaced by fine, new structures, but other slum areas remain. Washington has plans under consideration to improve the worst of its slums through its multi-million-dollar Model Cities program.

Another area slated for rehabilitation is Pennsylvania Avenue between the Capitol and the White House, where blocks of unattractive buildings line the north side of the nation's ceremonial street. That portion of the avenue will be transformed into the grand thoroughfare of L'Enfant's original plan, with broad sidewalks and rows of trees. On the north side of the avenue new Federal, municipal, and privately owned buildings will rise to balance the buildings of the Federal triangle across the street. A large reflecting pool at the head of the Mall will mirror the Capitol dome, and a mile away a national square will provide a suitably ceremonious approach to the

White House. The square will feature a 150-foot-wide fountain and a stately White House gate to be erected at Fifteenth Street. Midway between the Capitol and the White House, from Seventh to Ninth streets, a new market square will add variety to the avenue. The square will be tree-shaded and equipped with outdoor refreshment accommodations.

Plans are also under consideration for improving Washington's venerable Mall. They call for the addition of trees, fountains, kiosks, restaurants, bandstands, carrousels, playgrounds, sculptures, and outdoor exhibits to make the Mall a lively, exciting place.

When the plans for the Mall and those for Pennsylvania Avenue and the rest of the city have been carried out, the Washington of the Capitol, the White House, and the glistening marble memorials to the nation's heroes will be an even more beautiful Federal city for all Americans to enjoy.

The garden behind the Old Stone House has been replanted with thyme, rosemary, lavender, bee balm, and other herbs that grew there in colonial times.

Georgetown's many small shops specialize in antiques, art, clothing, and jewelry. The main shopping centers are on M Street and on Wisconsin Avenue.

This house on Thirty-first Street with its door lamp, shutters, and wrought iron railings helps give Georgetown its colonial atmosphere.

Opposite top
Dumbarton Oaks at 3101 R Street in Georgetown dates from 1801, although it has undergone extensive alterations since then. The mansion is now the property of Harvard University and the home of its Dumbarton Oaks Research Library and Collection, specializing in the arts of the early Christian, Byzantine, and pre-Colombian periods.

Opposite bottom
The R Street entrance to Dumbarton Oaks leads to the house through a grove of the oak trees that gave Dumbarton Oaks its name.

The formal gardens at Dumbarton Oaks are famous for their beauty. Dumbarton Oaks is open daily from 2 until 5 P.M. (The Museum is closed on Mondays.)

Built by William Thornton, the Capitol architect, and finished in 1800, distinguished Octagon House, at 1741 New York Avenue N.W., is now the national headquarters of the American Institute of Architects. Octagon House was President Madison's home for one year after the British burned the White House in 1814.

Washington is well supplied with hotels to accommodate its many visitors. This is the popular Mayflower on Connecticut Avenue at DeSales Street N.W., five blocks northeast of the White House. President Calvin Coolidge held his inaugural ball at the Mayflower, and numerous VIP's have attended functions there. The hotel has one thousand guest rooms.

The Shoreham Hotel and Motor Inn on Connecticut Avenue at Calvert Street N.W. overlooks Rock Creek Park. It offers its summer visitors horseback riding in the park, outdoor dining, a large swimming pool, and a lovely rose garden.

One of Washington's new luxury hotels, the International Inn on Thomas Circle, features a swimming pool under a glass dome that can be opened in the summer and closed during cold weather. The hotel has four hundred guest rooms.

The Madison, at Fifteenth and M streets N.W., is an elegant new downtown hotel. Although its exterior architecture is modern, the Madison's interior has been handsomely decorated in the style of the early 1800's.

Five acres of beautiful grounds surround the Washington Hilton at 1919 Connecticut Avenue N.W. The hotel has twelve hundred guest rooms and extensive convention facilities.

Anderson Cottage at the United States Soldiers' Home was President Lincoln's summer White House in 1864. More than two thousand retired and disabled Army and Air Force veterans live at the Soldiers' Home.

This is the Winfield Scott Building at the Soldiers' Home as it appears from Anderson Cottage.

The huge District of Columbia National Guard Armory at 2001 East Capitol Street has been the scene of Presidential inaugural balls and numerous successful trade shows.

Home of the Washington Senators of the American League and the Washington Redskins of the National Football League, the District of Columbia Stadium cost $19.8 million to build. The stadium, which opened in 1961, is located at Twenty-second and East Capitol streets.

When this picture was taken, a baseball game was under way in D.C. Stadium. The stadium can seat 45,000 for baseball and 50,000 for football. It has a ninety-two-acre parking lot.

One of Washington's new and distinctive office buildings, the National Geographic Society's headquarters at Seventeenth and M streets N.W., features a close fence of white-marble fins that terminate in a wide, slotted canopy. The building provides office space for six hundred National Geographic Society employees.

A globe that measures eleven feet from Pole to Pole revolves above a black-granite reflecting pool and fountain in the Explorers Hall of the National Geographic Building. The globe normally rotates on its axis, but an operator at a nearby console can move it in other directions to show any part of the earth's surface.

Memorial Continental Hall, National Headquarters of the Daughters of the American Revolution at Seventeenth and C streets N.W., is part of a full city block of DAR buildings. Continental Hall contains an outstanding genealogical library and a number of authentically furnished period rooms. Behind Continental Hall, with an entrance at 1776 D Street, is the DAR Museum and Administration Building.

Every spring, the members of the DAR gather in the organization's handsome Constitution Hall at 1778 D Street for a week of speeches and meetings. The building also serves as a Washington cultural center.

Constitution Hall's elegantly decorated auditorium seats four thousand persons. Many of the country's leading musical artists have performed here.

The American Red Cross has had its national headquarters at Seventeenth and D streets N.W. since 1917, when the building on the left was completed and dedicated to the heroic women of the Civil War. In addition to offices, it contains an assembly hall, library, and museum.

Blending the architectural styles of North and South America, the white marble Pan American Union Building at Seventeenth Street and Constitution Avenue N.W. serves as headquarters for the Organization of American States. The building, which is open to the public daily, except Sunday, contains a patio with tropical plants and birds, an art gallery, a Hall of Heroes decorated with busts of famous Americans and flags of American countries, and a Hall of the Americas, an ornate room used for concerts, receptions, and conferences. Behind the building a statue of Xochipilli, the Aztec god of flowers, is the focus of a beautiful Aztec garden.

The palatial French Embassy at 2221 Kalorama Road N.W. was once the home of John Hays Hammond, a Washingtonian who made a large fortune as a mining engineer.

The Italian Embassy at 1601 Fuller Street N.W. is in the Italian Renaissance style with a formal walled garden in the rear.

In this view of the window-walled Danish Embassy, the Ambassador's residence is on the left and the chancery, or diplomatic office building, is on the right. The building is located at 3200 Whitehaven Street N.W.

This building at 3401 Massachusetts Avenue N.W., near the Naval Observatory, has housed the Norwegian Embassy since 1932.

Finland's flag waves outside its chancery at 1900 Twenty-fourth Street N.W.

The Royal Netherlands Embassy conducts its business in a modern chancery at 4200 Linnean Avenue N.W.

The Netherlands Ambassador lives in this imposing residence at 2347 S Street N.W.

A rare sixteenth-century Gobelin tapestry hangs in the Netherlands Ambassador's entrance hall. The wooden statue on the table is by an unknown fifteenth-century Dutch artist.

Officially opened on May 11, 1964, and much admired for its architectural style, the chancery of the Federal Republic of Germany at 4645 Reservoir Road N.W. houses 140 offices, a 200-seat auditorium, a conference room, and a small cafeteria. The award-winning glass, wood, and steel building was designed by Egon Eiermann. The residence of the German Ambassador is near the chancery.

Located on a Virginia hillside directly across the Potomac River from the Lincoln Memorial, Arlington National Cemetery overlooks the river and the city of Washington.

10
NEARBY IN VIRGINIA AND MARYLAND

LIKE MANY OTHER AMERICAN CITIES, Washington has spilled over its official boundaries into the surrounding countryside. It is difficult to tell where the sixty-nine square miles that make up the District of Columbia end and Maryland begins. Even the Potomac River, that marks the District's southwestern boundary with Virginia, has not stopped the spread of the city. Politically, the areas outside the District boundaries have retained their independence, but from the air they appear to be part of Washington. Furthermore, a great many of the inhabitants of the outlying areas work in Washington and look to Washington for entertainment and other facilities. Nearby Virginia and Maryland have attractions of their own, however, and almost all visitors to the Capital include at least one or two of them in their itinerary.

Easily visible from the Lincoln Memorial, Arlington National Cemetery occupies 420 acres of gently rolling Virginia hillside bordering the Potomac River. Arlington is the most famous of all the cemeteries that are set aside for the nation's military dead. The Unknown Soldiers of World War I, World War II, and Korea are buried in Arlington graves, watched over by a solitary guard of honor who paces back and forth before the white marble Tomb of

the Unknown Soldier. On all sides, marked by simple headstones and more elaborate memorials, are the graves of soldiers, sailors, airmen, and marines of all ranks. Two Presidents of the United States, John F. Kennedy and William Howard Taft, are buried in Arlington.

The stately Custis-Lee mansion on its hill overlooking the cemetery and the Potomac is a reminder of Arlington's past. It was once part of an estate that belonged to George Washington Parke Custis, the grandson of Martha Washington and the adopted son of George Washington. Custis built his hilltop house between 1802 and 1817. When his daughter married Lieutenant Robert E. Lee in 1831, Arlington became their home. At the outbreak of the Civil War, Lee, by then a colonel, resigned his commission in the United States Army to join the Confederate forces. Shortly thereafter, Arlington was occupied by Union soldiers, and part of its grounds became a military cemetery.

In 1883, the United States Government paid $150,000 for legal title to Arlington, which had continued in use as a cemetery; however, the mansion remained empty until 1925 except for the part used as cemetery offices. Since then, restored to the elegance it knew as the home of the Custis and Lee families, it has become one of the major attractions of the nearby Virginia area.

South of the Capital, the Virginia side of the Potomac River is rich in associations with George Washington. He called Alexandria, Virginia, his home town. It was there that he bought supplies for Mount Vernon, visited his many friends, and went to church.

Like Georgetown, Alexandria predates the founding of the Capital, and, also like Georgetown, it became a prosperous tobacco port on the Potomac River. Alexandria has even more fine old structures remaining than does Georgetown, and its narrow, tree-lined streets retain a charming, colonial air.

Alexandria's Christ Church, at 118 North Washington Street, was built between 1767 and 1773, and it looks much the same today as it did when George Washington was a vestryman there. He rented pew number 60. Robert E. Lee was another of Christ Church's famous parishioners.

During the French and Indian War, General Braddock planned his disastrous campaign of 1775 at Carlyle House, a Georgian colonial mansion that still stands at 121 North Fairfax Street. George Washington visited Carlyle House both as a member of Braddock's staff and at other times as well, because the house became a gathering place for Revolutionary leaders. It is now open to the public as a museum.

Another famous old Alexandria building that has become a museum is Gadsby's Tavern, at 132 North Royal Street. Gadsby's, which opened in 1752, was probably the best-known tavern in colonial America. George Washington used it as his headquarters during the French and Indian War, and, in 1799, attended his last birthday party there.

The first President's memorial in Alexandria, the George Washington Masonic National Memorial, stands on Shooters Hill, a site once proposed for the United States Capitol. In design, the towering memorial resembles the ancient Pharos Lighthouse that once stood in Alexandria, Egypt. Included in the memorial's many items connected with George Washington are some associated with his Masonic membership. He was the first master of the Masonic Lodge of Alexandria.

Washington's home at Mount Vernon is seven miles south of Alexandria, at the end of the scenic Mount Vernon Memorial Highway. When Washington lived there, Mount Vernon was a large estate divided into five farms on which he grew tobacco and other crops. The house at Mount Vernon occupies part of what was his Mansion House Farm.

George Washington inherited Mount Vernon from his half-brother Lawrence in 1752, when the house was much smaller than it is now. Although his duties first as a soldier and later as President of the United States kept him away from Mount Vernon for long periods, Washington enlarged and improved the house several times. He also took an active interest in the crops that were raised on his farms. At the time of his death in 1799, Mount Vernon was an elegantly furnished mansion with beautiful gardens and an unsurpassed view of the Potomac River from its broad veranda.

Unfortunately, Washington's heirs were unable to maintain Mount Vernon, and for some years they were unable to sell it. Finally, in 1856, a group of patriotic women banded together as the Mount Vernon Ladies' Association to save the first President's home. During the next few years they raised $200,000, enough to buy the house and part of the old Mansion House Farm. Since then the association has restored the house and the grounds, now extended to about five hundred acres. Their admirable restoration project has included not only the physical repair of the property, but also the return to Mount Vernon of many of George and Martha Washington's possessions. As a result, Mount Vernon gives its millions of visitors an understanding of the first President and his way of life that is to be found in no other memorial.

Although it was built after his death, Woodlawn, another historic Virginia house, has close associations with George Washington. It belonged to his favorite nephew, Lawrence Lewis, who married Martha Washington's granddaughter, Eleanor Custis. The first President gave land to them from his Mount Vernon estate, and his friend William Thornton, the Capitol architect, designed the Georgian mansion which was completed in 1805. The restored house, located on U.S. Highway 1 three miles south of Mount Vernon, is administered by the National Trust for Historic Preservation and is open to the public daily.

About four miles south of Woodlawn, on U.S.

Highway 1, Pohick Church testifies to George Washington's ability as an architect. He served on the building committee when the church was erected between 1769 and 1774, and tradition has it that he drew the ground plan and an elevation for the church using Christ Church in Alexandria as a model. The restored building is still in use as an Episcopal church.

Farther away, on a Virginia hilltop about 110 miles southwest of Washington, is a beautiful memorial to the third President of the United States, his own beloved home, Monticello. Thomas Jefferson designed Monticello himself and supervised its construction. When he married in 1772, the house was still unfinished, and for several months he lived with his bride in a cottage while work went forward on the main house. The cottage was later incorporated into the south terrace.

Jefferson's Monticello is one of the finest examples of the classical revival style in America. Its pedimented portico and evenly balanced design are still much admired, and its interior has several interesting innovations devised by the third President. His hall clock has two dials, the second one outside on the portico. The clock's cannonball weights indicate the day of the week as they move past markers on the wall. The ladder that Jefferson climbed to wind the clock folds up into a pole when not in use. The double doors leading from the hall into the drawing room both open or close when one is moved. In the dining room, miniature dumb-waiters are concealed in the fireplace mantel, and Jefferson attached shelves to a revolving door to facilitate food-serving.

Like his friend George Washington, Jefferson was often away from his home, but he, too, managed to carry on extensive remodeling projects, and he kept a close check on the development of the grounds and the four large farms that made up Monticello.

Jefferson died at Monticello on July 4, 1826, at the age of eighty-two. Soon afterward the house and its contents had to be sold to settle claims against the estate. Like Mount Vernon, Monticello was neglected for many years until a group of public-spirited citizens came to its rescue.

The Thomas Jefferson Memorial Foundation bought Monticello in 1923 after a funds drive to which people all over the United States contributed their nickels, dimes, and dollars. Since then the foundation has restored the house and grounds and reequipped Monticello with some of Jefferson's furniture. Today, Monticello, generally considered one of the most beautiful houses in the United States, looks much as it did when Jefferson lived there.

The Maryland side of the District of Columbia has its own associations with the nation's past. The area is rich in colonial history, and Annapolis, Maryland's capital located about thirty miles east of Washington, was for a short time after the Revolutionary War the Capital of the United States. Since 1845, the lovely colonial city on the Severn River has been the home of the United States Naval Academy.

While Maryland communities are justifiably proud of their past, several of them have also achieved prominence because of their strictly twentieth-century research organizations, some of them operated by the Federal Government. One of the largest is the National Institutes of Health in suburban Bethesda, Maryland, headquarters for a large-scale Federal effort to investigate a wide variety of diseases, with the aim of controlling or eliminating them. Seven of the nine separate institutes that make up the National Institutes of Health work on the problems caused by cancer, cardiovascular and geriatric diseases, allergies and infectious diseases, arthritic and metabolic diseases, dental diseases, mental illnesses, and neurological and sensory diseases. An eighth institute deals with general medical problems, and a ninth concentrates on child health and human growth.

Across Wisconsin Avenue from the National Institutes of Health, the United States Navy operates another large medical research facility. The National Naval Medical Center also conducts training courses for naval personnel and treats patients in its large hospital.

At Greenbelt, Maryland, the National Aeronautics and Space Administration's Goddard Space Flight Center develops unmanned satellites and conducts research with them. Its highly sophisticated computers supply tracking and other information in support of NASA's space exploration activities. The Department of Agriculture operates a large research center at Beltsville with laboratories and other facilities for conducting experiments aimed at improving plants, livestock, and poultry. The National Bureau of Standards, the government agency responsible for basic measurement standards and research leading to new and improved industrial products, is located at Gaithersburg, Maryland. These and other government and private research organizations have brought large numbers of doctors, physicists, and other scientists to the Washington area.

Because National Airport, just across the Potomac River from Washington, was too small and crowded to handle the Capital's air traffic, the Federal Aviation Agency opened a large, new airport near Chantilly, Virginia, in 1962. Named Dulles International Airport, for John Foster Dulles, President Dwight D. Eisenhower's much-traveled Secre-

tary of State, the airport, with its modern terminal and mobile lounges to carry passengers to their planes and long runways, was designed specifically for jet travel. The terminal and control tower at Dulles are outstanding examples of contemporary architecture. A landscaped parkway connects the airport with Washington. Conventional aircraft and small jets continue to use National Airport, and Friendship International Airport, near Baltimore, Maryland, handles some of the city's air traffic, but Dulles, in its design and purpose, is the airport that symbolizes Washington's position as the Capital of a nation whose influence extends to the four corners of the world.

Preeminent among Arlington National Cemetery's many memorials is the Tomb of the Unknown Soldier, an impressive white marble block erected in 1931 to mark the grave of an unknown World War I soldier. Unidentified dead of World War II and the Korean war were later buried at his side.

Day and night, in good weather and bad, an armed sentry guards the Tomb of the Unknown Soldier. The guards, members of the elite First Battle Group of the Third Infantry Regiment stationed at nearby Fort Myer, are replaced every hour during a changing of the guard ceremony.

The Arlington Memorial Amphitheatre, located a few feet west of the Tomb of the Unknown Soldier, was finished in 1920 and dedicated to Army, Navy, and Marine Corps dead. The white marble amphitheatre, which seats about four thousand people, is used for Easter sunrise, Memorial Day, and Veterans' Day services.

Frequent signs help the visitor find his way along the roads and paths that wind through the 420 acres that make up Arlington National Cemetery. The equestrian statue on the right marks the grave of Civil War General Philip Kearny.

Six hundred graves of soldiers who served in that war surround Arlington's Spanish-American War monument, a tall granite shaft surmounted by an eagle. This is one of several Arlington monuments honoring special groups of soldiers and sailors.

Top right
Seven marble stairs lead to President Kennedy's grave, which is marked by a slate stone bearing his name. The eternal flame burns behind the grave.

A simple two-foot wooden cross marks the Arlington grave of Senator Robert F. Kennedy, the brother of President John F. Kennedy. Senator Kennedy was assassinated in 1968 while campaigning in California for the Democratic Presidential nomination.

Millions of Americans have visited the Arlington grave of John F. Kennedy, the thirty-fifth President of the United States, who was assassinated in 1963. The circular grave site on a grassy hillside overlooking Washington is surrounded by rows of the cemetery's white markers. The Custis-Lee Mansion is at left center.

The historic Custis-Lee Mansion occupies one of the highest points in Arlington National Cemetery. Now administered by the National Park Service, the authentically restored house and its grounds are open to the public from 9:30 A.M. until 4:30 P.M. daily (open until 6 P.M. from April through September).

At night, the impressive, flood-lighted portico of the Custis-Lee Mansion is visible from many parts of Washington. From the portico daytime visitors to the mansion can enjoy a magnificent view of the Potomac River and Washington.

Restored after 1925 following years of neglect, the Custis-Lee Mansion is now furnished in the style of the first half of the nineteenth century. Many of the present furnishings were in the house when the Custis and Lee families lived there.

The Capitol, the Washington Monument, and the Lincoln Memorial form a backdrop for the heroic Marine Corps War Memorial honoring the men who fought on the Pacific island of Iwo Jima during World War II, and all Marines who have given their lives for their country since the Corps was founded in 1775. The sculptured rendition of the raising of the American flag on Iwo Jima's Mount Suribachi was based on one of World War II's most famous combat photographs. The memorial occupies a hilltop north of Arlington National Cemetery near the Virginia end of Memorial Bridge.

The thirty-two-foot figures of the Marine Corps War Memorial tower above a Marine bugler taking part in a ceremony at the memorial. At 7:30 P.M. on Tuesdays during the summer months, the Marine Corps Drum and Bugle Corps, Ceremonial Battalion, and Color Guard honor Marine dead from all wars in an impressive ceremony at the memorial.

Financed by Masons all over the United States, the 333-foot George Washington Masonic National Memorial soars over Alexandria, Virginia. The memorial contains an outstanding collection of Washington memorabilia, including the Washington family Bible, the trowel used by the first President when he laid the cornerstone of the Capitol, and the clock from his bedroom, stopped at 10:20, the time of his death on December 14, 1799. Washington served as first master of the Masonic Lodge of Alexandria. The memorial is open from 9 A.M. until 5 P.M. daily.

The Mount Vernon Memorial Highway between Arlington Memorial Bridge and Mount Vernon provides one of the most scenic drives in the Washington area. The highway follows the Virginia shore of the Potomac River, and passes through miles of countryside associated with George Washington.

"No estate in United America is more pleasantly situated than this." That is how George Washington described Mount Vernon in a letter to an English friend. Washington's stately hilltop home, now a memorial to the first President, is open to the public every day of the year from 9 A.M.

From the high-columned piazza that extends the full length of the house, the Washingtons and their many guests enjoyed a fine view of the Potomac River and the distant Maryland hills.

Opposite bottom
Another way to explore the Potomac between Washington and Mount Vernon is aboard a Wilson Line excursion boat that makes regularly scheduled trips to Mount Vernon during the warm weather months. The Wilson Line's Washington terminal is Pier 4 on the Maine Avenue waterfront.

197

Mount Vernon's Banquet Hall has been carefully restored to look just as it did when George and Martha Washington entertained friends there. The Palladian window shown here is one of the mansion's many striking architectural features.

This staircase leads to Mount Vernon's second floor where five bedchambers and Washington's own sleeping quarters contain furniture and other objects associated with the first President and his family.

It was George Washington's wish that he be buried at his beloved Mount Vernon, and his will contained directions for the building of the vault that contains his remains and those of Martha Washington and other relatives. The tomb is located on a bluff above the Potomac River.

At the National Institutes of Health in Bethesda, Maryland, a Washington suburb, federally financed research in nine major areas of medicine is being carried out by a large staff of scientists and doctors. This photograph shows some of the buildings on the campus-like National Institutes grounds.

The National Library of Medicine occupies a modern building in the National Institutes of Health compound. The library, which has the largest and best collection of medical literature in the world, serves as a national source for medical information.

In the tall tower and wings of its National Naval Medical Center in Bethesda, the United States Navy conducts medical research, trains medical and dental personnel, and cares for patients, many of whom are flown to Bethesda for specialized treatment from naval installations all over the world.

The main offices of the Atomic Energy Commission are located in the gently rolling countryside near Germantown, Maryland, about twenty miles northwest of Washington. The commission administers United States programs for research, development, and production in the fields of atomic energy and special nuclear materials.

Above Washington, the Potomac River becomes narrow and its irregular course is strewn with rocks. This is a popular scenic and recreation area.

In the spring and fall the Roaches Run Waterfowl Sanctuary provides a safe resting place for migrating wild ducks. The sanctuary is on the Virginia side of the Potomac River across from East Potomac Park.

Thomas Jefferson's lovely home, Monticello, testifies to his ability as an architect and inventor. The Thomas Jefferson Memorial Foundation has restored the house and furnished it with many items that belonged to the third President. Monticello, located four miles southeast of Charlottesville, Virginia, is open to the public daily from 8 A.M. until 5 P.M. (until 4:30 P.M., November through March).

Thomas Jefferson kept this small pond at Monticello stocked with edible fish. He thought of himself as a farmer and laid out his lawns and gardens with great care. The lawns near the house have been restored according to Jefferson's plans.

Washington National Airport, just across the Potomac River in Virginia, is only three miles from the heart of the city. Its busy runways handle conventional aircraft and small jets.

Ever since it opened in 1940, Washington National Airport has been one of the country's most used air terminals. The airport was built on land reclaimed from the Potomac River.

Mobile lounges carry passengers from the terminal building at Dulles to airplanes parked some distance away. The airport, with its roads, runways, and buildings, covers ten thousand acres, making it the largest airport in the United States.

Opposite top
Dulles International Airport, Washington's jet-age airport, was the first in the United States to be designed specifically for jet travelers. Its architect, Eero Saarinen, designed the terminal building and the control tower to convey both the excitement of travel and the stateliness of belonging to the Federal Capital. Dulles Airport is twenty-seven miles west of Washington.

Opposite bottom
The hammock-like suspension roof of the Dulles terminal building covers a large concourse whose facilities were planned with the needs of incoming and outgoing passengers in mind.

INDEX

INDEX

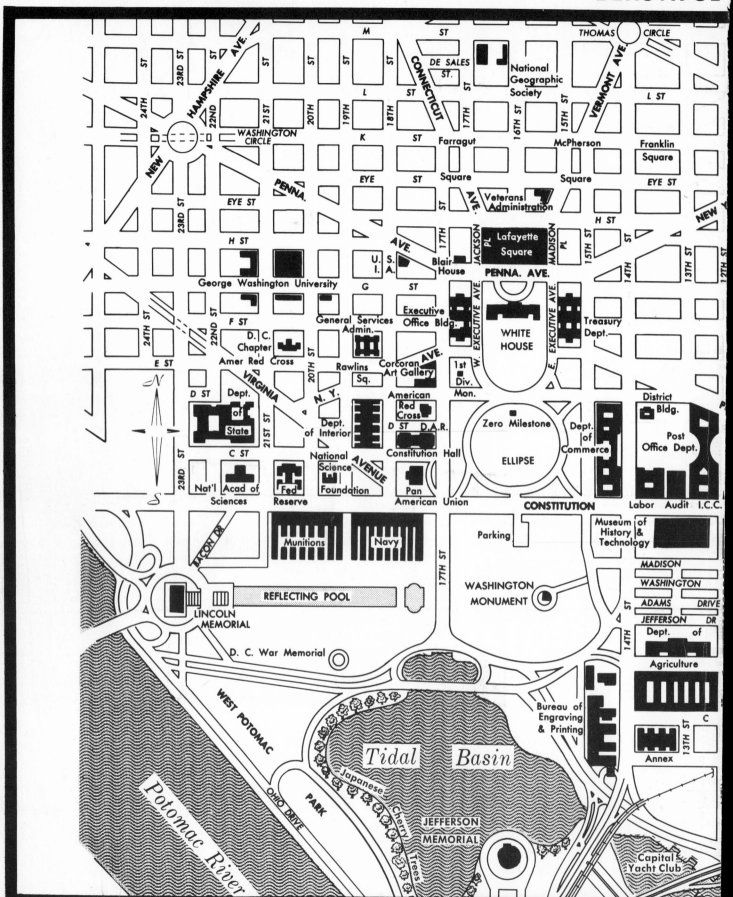

Courtesy, National Park Service, U.S. Department of the Interior